AF593762

The Fujica SLR Book

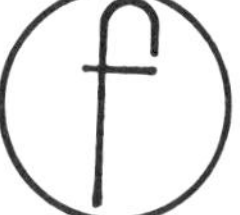

FOCAL CAMERA BOOKS

THE ASAHI PENTAX BOOK	*Clyde Reynolds*
THE ASAHI PENTAX BOOK M & K RANGE	*Clyde Reynolds*
THE CANON SLR BOOK	*Leonard Gaunt*
THE CONTAX & YASHICA SLR BOOK	*Clyde Reynolds*
THE FUJICA SLR BOOK	*Leonard Gaunt*
THE KONICA AUTOREFLEX BOOK	*Paul Petzold*
THE MAMIYA BOOK	*Clyde Reynolds*
THE MINOLTA XE-1 & SR-T BOOK	*Clyde Reynolds*
THE NIKON BOOK	*Clyde Reynolds*
THE NIKKORMAT BOOK	*Clyde Reynolds*
THE OLYMPUS BOOK	*Leonard Gaunt*
THE PRAKTICA BOOK	*Leonard Gaunt*
THE ZORKI & FED BOOK	*Leonard Gaunt*

FOCAL CAMERA GUIDES

ASAHI PENTAX GUIDE 20th ed.	*W. D. Emanuel*
CANONET GUIDE 6th ed.	*W. D. Emanuel*
CANON REFLEX GUIDE 6th ed.	*W. D. Emanuel*
EXAKTA 35 mm GUIDE 10th ed.	*W. D. Emanuel*
HASSELBLAD GUIDE 4th ed.	*W. D. Emanuel*
KONICA COMPACT 35 mm GUIDE 1st ed.	*W. D. Emanuel*
KONICA REFLEX GUIDE 7th ed.	*W. D. Emanuel*
LEICA GUIDE 44th ed.	*W. D. Emanuel*
LEICAFLEX GUIDE 4th ed.	*A. Matheson*
MAMIYA SEKOR GUIDE 4th ed.	*W. D. Emanuel*
MINOLTA SR GUIDE 9th ed.	*W. D. Emanuel*
MINOX GUIDE 9th ed.	*W. D. Emanuel*
NIKON F GUIDE 6th ed.	*W. D. Emanuel*
NIKKORMAT GUIDE 7th ed.	*W. D. Emanuel*
OLYMPUS OM-1 GUIDE 4th ed.	*W. D. Emanuel*
OLYMPUS 35 mm COMPACT GUIDE 2nd ed.	*W. D. Emanuel*
PRAKTICA PRAKTICAMAT GUIDE 8th ed.	*W. D. Emanuel*
RETINETTE GUIDE 8th ed.	*W. D. Emanuel*
ROLLEIFLEX GUIDE 40th ed.	*W. D. Emanuel*
ROLLEI 35 mm GUIDE 3rd ed.	*W. D. Emanuel*
YASHICA 35 mm GUIDE 5th ed.	*W. D. Emanuel*
YASHICA TWIN LENS REFLEX GUIDE 7th ed.	*W. D. Emanuel*

CAMERA WAY BOOKS

THE ASAHI PENTAX WAY 10th ed.	*Herbert Keppler*
THE CANON REFLEX WAY 2nd ed.	*Leonard Gaunt*
THE HASSELBLAD WAY 7th ed.	*H. Freytag*
THE LEICA & LEICAFLEX WAY 11th ed.	*Andrew Matheson*
THE NIKON/NIKKORMAT WAY 2nd ed.	*Herbert Keppler*
THE PRAKTICA WAY 4th ed.	*Leonard Gaunt*
THE RETINA WAY 10th ed.	*O. R. Croy*
THE ROLLEI WAY 9th ed.	*L. A. Mannheim*
THE ROLLEIFLEX SL66 & SLX WAY 1st ed.	*L. A. Mannheim*

This book is sold subject to the Standard Conditions of Sale of Net Books and may not be re-sold in the UK below the net price.

THE FUJICA SLR BOOK

for ST 901, 801, 705, 605 and AZ-1 users

LEONARD GAUNT

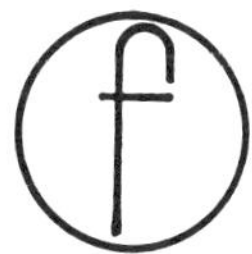

Focal Press • London

Focal/Hastings House • New York

© 1978 Focal Press Limited

All Rights Reserved. No part of this publication may be reproduced, stored in a retrieval system, or transmitted, in any form or by any means, electronic, mechanical, photocopying, recording or otherwise, without the prior permission of the Copyright owner.

BL British Library Cataloguing in Publication Data

GAUNT, LEONARD
The Fujica SLR book. (Focal camera books).
1. Fujica camera I. Title
771.3'1 TR263.F/
ISBN (excl USA) 0 240 50976 5
ISBN (USA only) 0 8038 2360 6

First edition 1978

Printed and bound in Great Britain at The Pitman Press, Bath.

Contents

Where to look for . . .

Single-lens reflex features

In a single-lens reflex camera the viewfinder image is formed by the camera lens. Thus, the viewfinder image is always the same, allowing for framing tolerances, as that which subsequently appears on the negative or slide. No separate viewfinder is necessary when the camera lens is changed or when attachments such as close-up lenses, extension tubes, bellows or tele-extenders are used.

In the older single-lens reflexes, this principle was simply achieved by placing a movable mirror at a 45 degree angle behind the lens to redirect the image through 90 degrees to a ground glass screen in the top of the camera. The mirror was so placed that the distance from its surface to the film and to the viewfinder screen were the same. Thus, the viewfinder screen could also be used for focusing. When the image was accurately focused on the screen it must also be in focus on the film.

Later refinements

This is still the basic principle that is used in the modern 35 mm single-lens reflex, although many refinements have been added. The 35 mm camera for example is nearly always used at eye level so an ingenious five-sided prism (pentaprism) was designed to sit on top of the focusing screen to turn the image-forming rays through another 90 degrees so that the user could look in the direction of the subject while he took his picture. But that is not all the pentaprism does. It also corrects the lateral reversal that would be present if simple mirrors were used, so that the viewer sees an upright, right-way-round image on his screen.

The final part of the 35 mm single-lens reflex viewing system is the eyepiece lens, focused on the viewfinder screen via the reflecting surfaces of the prism. This is a magnifying eyepiece which enables the viewer to see an image that appears nearly life size when the standard 50 mm lens is attached to the camera.

The 35 mm single-lens reflex

TOP

1 Subject
2 Lens
3 Diaphragm
4 Viewing and focusing screen
5 Pentaprism
6 Viewfinder eyepiece
7 Pressure plate
8 Mirror
9 Film
10 Image as seen through eyepiece

BOTTOM

The film used in the 35 mm single-lens reflex is 35 mm wide, perforated along both edges. The image size is normally 36 x 24 mm and generally includes fractionally more than is visible in the viewfinder.

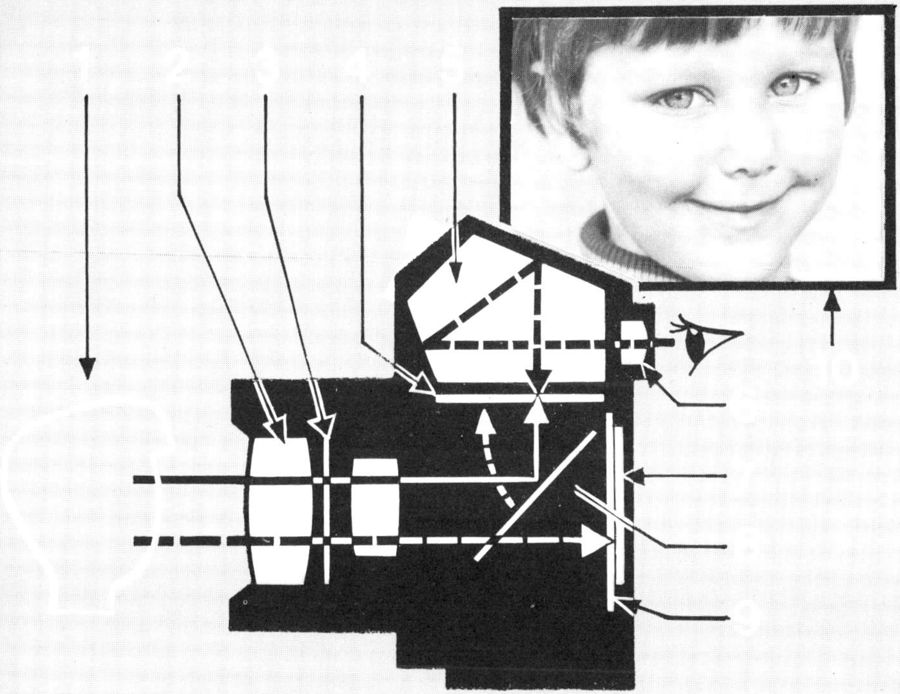

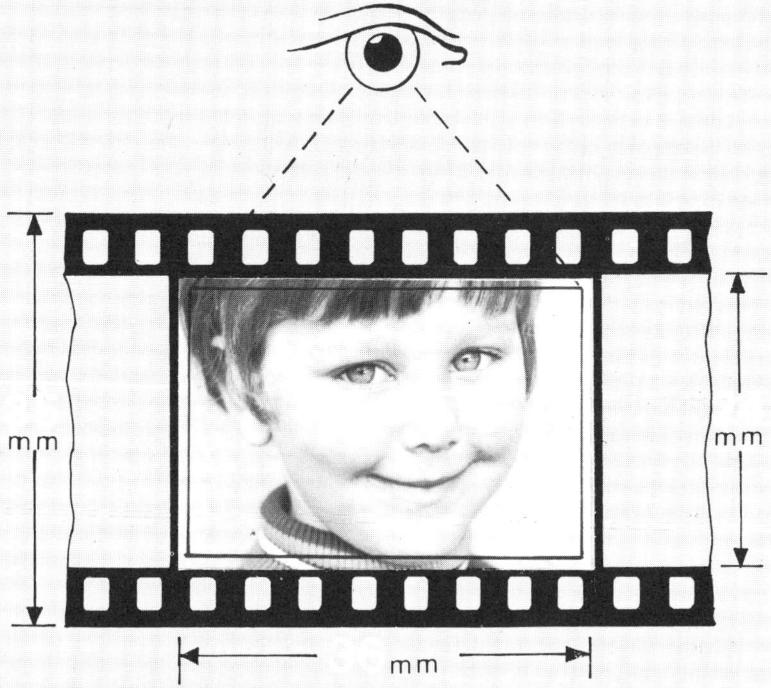

1
2
3
4
5
10
9
mm
mm
mm

Single-lens reflex operation

The main refinements that have been added to the original single-lens reflex design are the instant return mirror and the automatic diaphragm. Early cameras of this type were rather slow in operation and a little disconcerting to the user. Although the mirror automatically flipped up out of the light path when the shutter release was pressed, it stayed there, blacking out the view through the eyepiece until the film was wound on for the next exposure – an operation that also tensioned the shutter.

Similarly, as it is always advisable to view and focus the image at its brightest, the user had constantly to open and close the lens diaphragm between shots. Inevitably, he frequently forgot to stop down after focusing and overexposed his film by shooting unintentionally at full aperture.

The modern single lens reflex overcomes both of these problems. The mirror not only rises automatically just before the shutter opens but also returns to the viewing position when the shutter closes. The viewfinder blackout is barely noticeable at the faster shutter speeds.

The diaphragm setting problem was overcome by linking the operation with a simple push rod or sliding lever mechanism emerging from the back of the lens mount. Pushing the pin inward or the lever sideways closes diaphragm down, either by direct action or by releasing a spring mechanism in the lens. Thus, a simple link in the camera body connected to the shutter release stops down the lens automatically while the shutter is open and lets it return to full aperture when the shutter closed.

Sequence of operations

The complete single lens reflex operation is:

1 The picture is composed and focused on the viewfinder screen with the mirror down and the lens at full aperture.

2 The aperture control ring is set to the required shooting aperture and the shutter release depressed. The lens diaphragm stops down to the pre-set aperture, the mirror rises and the shutter opens.

3 The shutter closes, the mirror returns to the viewing position and the lens diaphragm returns to the fully open position. The pre-set aperture remains and when the shutter release is pressed again, the diaphragm again stops down to that aperture.

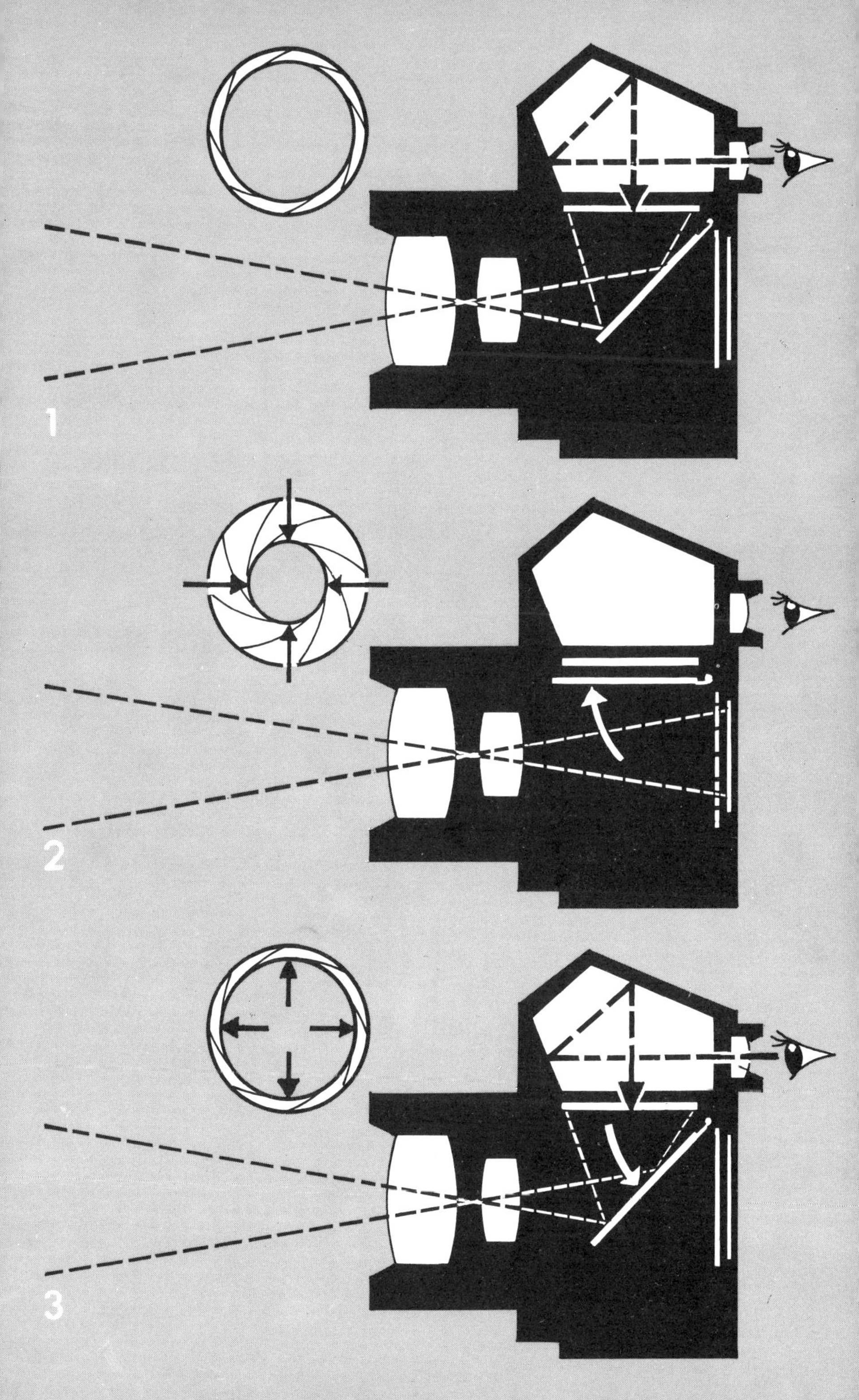

1
2
3

The Fujica SLR cameras

The Fujica SLR models are all 35mm single lens reflexes with through the lens exposure meters. Each, although obviously belonging to the same family, has its individual characteristics, mainly in the type of metering or in the meter readout.

The ST605 is the basic model, with shutter speeds from 1/2 second to 1/700 second and stopped-down metering operated by a button switch on the camera front.

The ST705 is an upgraded version with speeds from 1 second to 1/1500 second and full-aperture metering operated by the first pressure on the shutter release.

The ST801 extends the shutter speed range still further – from 1 second to 1/2000 second. It is most noteworthy, however, for its meter readout, which uses seven light-emitting diodes (LEDs) instead of a meter needle.

The ST901, the most sophisticated version, has an electronic shutter controlled by the metering system to give shutter speeds from 20 seconds to 1/1000 second in a continuously variable range. It can be used manually at the orthodox speeds from 1/60 to 1/1000 second. The meter readout is digital, indicating the range within which the meter will set the shutter speed when the shutter release is fully depressed.

The AZ-1 is also an automatic-exposure model with electronically-controlled shutter but shutter speeds run only from 1/2 to 1/1000 second in the normal steps. It can be used manually at speeds of 1/60, 1/250 and 1/1000 second. The meter readout is by a series of LEDs indicating the shutter speed selected by the meter circuit. Sustained first pressure on the shutter release locks the exposure setting. An auto winder is available.

All the cameras take universal 42mm-thread lenses and attachments but the full-aperture metering facility is retained only with lenses specifically made for the Fujica cameras. These lenses have a recess to accept the locking pin on the lens flange and a lug to move the full-aperture teller surrounding the flange.

Accessories include one or two unusual items (see pages 14 and 106) and, of course, innumerable other accessories with 42mm threads can be used.

Batteries

All the camera metering systems are battery powered, the 605 and 705 by two 1.5 volt silver oxide batteries, the 801 and 901 by one 6 volt silver oxide or manganese alkaline battery and the AZ-1 by three 1.5 volt silver oxide batteries. The cameras can be operated without batteries at all shutter speeds but with no metering facility, except the 901 and AZ-1 which have limited ranges of manually-set shutter speeds.

The battery compartment is to the left of the viewfinder eyepiece on all models. Access is obtained by unscrewing the cover. On the 605 and 705, load the batteries with the plus sign facing you. The 801 and 901 use the same type of single six volt battery but on the 901 it loads with the plus (positive) end up while on the 801 it loads with the minus (negative) end facing you. The three batteries of the AZ-1 are loaded with plus (positive) side inward. Always remove the batteries if you expect not to use the camera for a prolonged period.

The Fujica models

All the Fujica SLRs bear a strong family resemblance
A AZ–1. **B** ST901. **C** ST801. **D** ST705. **E** ST605.

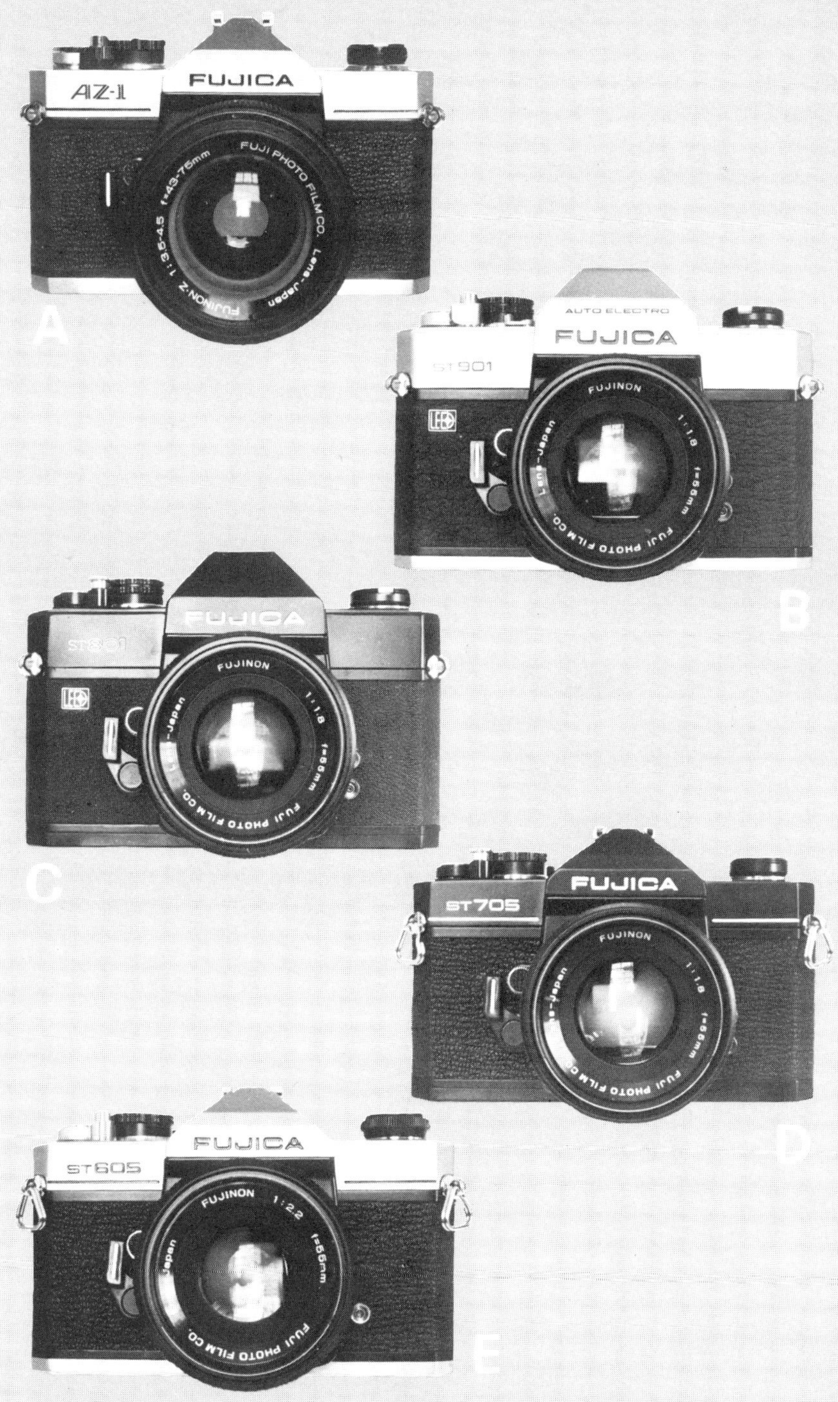
FUJICA
AZ-1
FUJI PHOTO FILM CO.
Lens-Japan
FUJINON·Z 1:3.5-4.5 f=43-75mm
A
AUTO ELECTRO
FUJICA
ST901
FUJINON 1:1.8 f=55mm
Lens-Japan
FUJI PHOTO FILM CO.
B
FUJICA
ST801
FUJINON 1:1.8 f=55mm
Lens-Japan
FUJI PHOTO FILM CO.
C
FUJICA
ST705
FUJINON 1:1.8 f=55mm
FUJI PHOTO FILM CO.
D
FUJICA
ST605
FUJINON 1:2.2 f=55mm
FUJI PHOTO FILM CO.
E

The Fujica system

The range of accessories provided specifically for the Fujica cameras is not extensive but it includes all the most frequently used items and a few interesting and unusual ones.

Close-up equipment

Single lens reflex cameras are particularly well suited to close-range work and there are accordingly several pieces of close-up equipment in the Fujica range. There is a close-up lens for attachment to the standard lens to allow shooting at 28–50 cm (11–19$\frac{1}{2}$ in). To get closer still, you can use extension tubes. The Fujica set of three tubes is in lengths of 9.5, 19 and 28 mm. Used together, with a standard lens, they give a more than life size image on the film. For even greater magnification in a continuously variable range there is an extension bellows. With either tubes or bellows you can use the Fujica reverse adapter to mount the lens back to front for macro work, or the Leica mount adapter in conjunction with Leica-screw enlarging or other lenses.

When photographing extremely small objects at large magnifications, it is better to use a microscope and attach it to the camera by the Fujica microscope adapter. Then, as with other close range work, you might also find it better to view the screen image from above or to one side of the camera. This you can do with the right-angle finder attached to the viewfinder eyepiece.

There is yet another copying accessory in the Fujica range – the Macrocinecopier, allowing you to copy single frames of 8 mm and 16 mm films and microscope slides.

Eyepiece attachments

If you find it difficult to see the screen image clearly, it is likely that you are too near- or far-sighted for the optical location of the screen. In that case you can fit an eyesight adjustment lens to the viewfinder eyepiece. Spectacle wearers might also find the eyecup useful. It blocks out extraneous light both from the screen and the meter sensors.

Other accessories

Naturally, you can use any other accessories with the universal 42 mm thread of the Fujinon lenses. There are various items made by other camera manufacturers and independent suppliers. Generally, the use of such equipment makes the full-aperture metering system inoperative but stopped down metering is always possible and the automatic diaphragm operation is usually retained.

An Auto Winder and automatic flash unit are available for the Fujica AZ-1.

The Fujica system

A Auto Strobo flashgun for AZ–1 fits to accessory shoe. Other flash units can be attached to accessory shoe or coaxial socket. **B** Eyepiece correction lenses. **C** Rightangle finder. **D** Close-up lens. **E** Filter. **F** Interchangeable lenses. **G** Bellows. **H** Reverse adapter. **J** Microscope adapter. **K** Extension tubes. **L** Macrocinecopy.

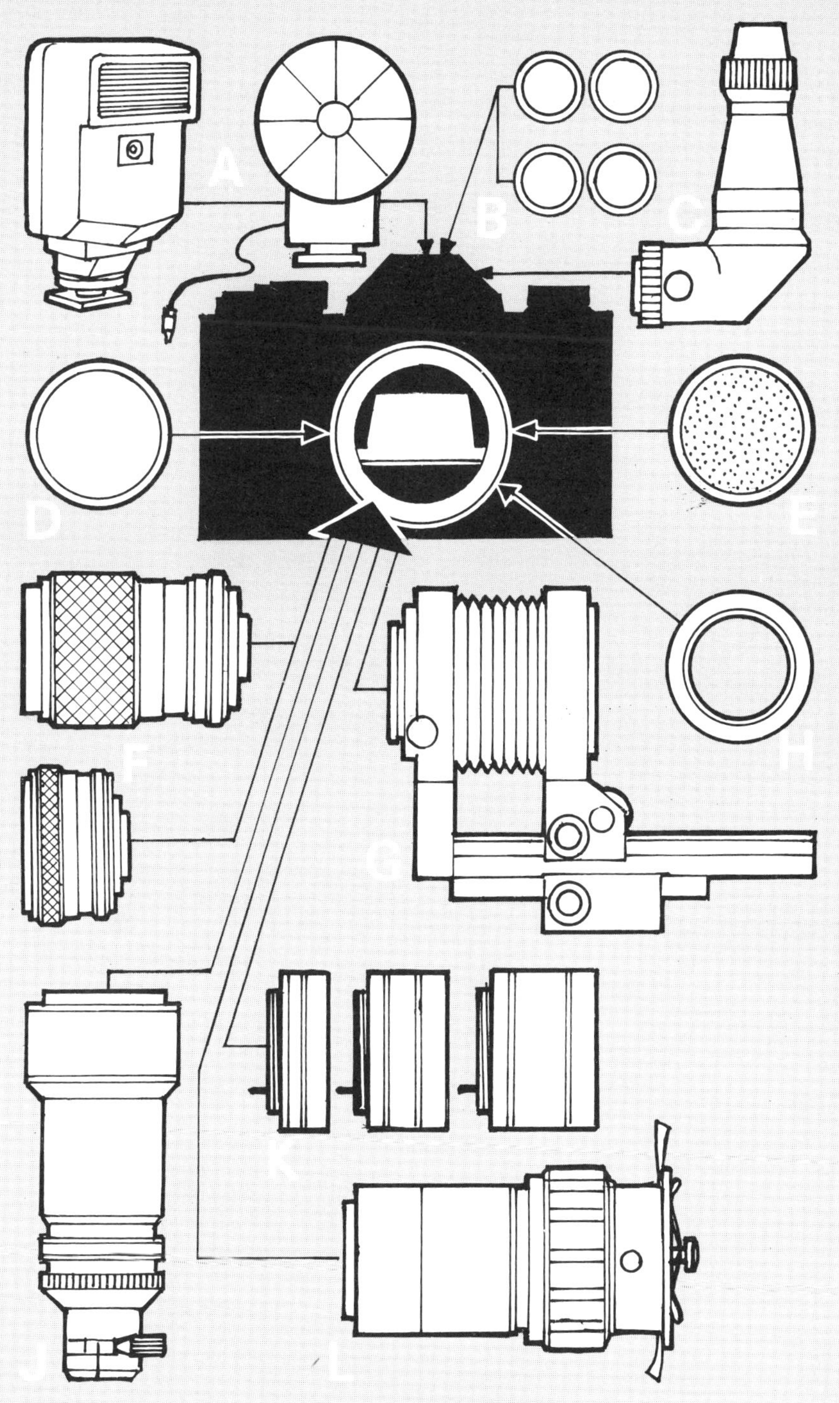
A
B
C
D
E
F
G
H
J
K
L

Building up a system

A "system" camera is only the basis of a system. The ease and efficiency with which you can deal with your picture taking depends largely on the accessories you select. An important factor in such selection must be portability. It is no good attempting nature photography if you can't carry your equipment without a car!

Lenses

Accessory lenses are an essential part of any system, but they should be selected with care, taking account of how they relate to one another and what other lenses you may need later. It is also important to choose a range which you can carry with you and which covers all your likely uses.

Most cameras are supplied with a standard lens, and others should normally be chosen to complement it. The most useful wide-angle to supplement this for the 35 mm photographer is probably a 28 mm, which gives greatly increased coverage and depth of field and can be used without the special care needed with ultrawide (15–25 mm) lenses. A suitable long-focus companion to these is a 100 to 150 mm lens. If you don't intend to buy any more long focus lenses, the choice will depend only on the expected uses. A lens of around 100 mm is best for portraits, but a longer one is probably more useful for picturing distant objects. For most photographers, 125 or 135 mm is a good compromise.

If you intend to build further, your first purchases should be considered more carefully. For example if you envisage using a 200 mm lens at some later date, a 100 mm would be a better choice than a 150 mm, whereas if you were contemplating a 300 mm lens, perhaps for sports photography, a 150 mm may be a better companion. Lenses much longer than 300 mm, or much shorter than 28 mm should only be considered for specialist purposes, and may be of less influence on your choice of general purpose lenses.

If you are starting from scratch you might consider buying a camera body without a standard lens, and then a selection of lenses. Thus you might choose a 35 mm and 85 mm to start, adding perhaps a 24 mm and 150 mm at a later date. This would be a particularly valuable saving if you ever intended buying a 50 mm macro lens, which makes a perfectly good "standard" lens.

There are two major types of lenses useful for increasing your versatility: teleconverters and zooms. The major disadvantage of teleconverters is that they reduce the light reaching the film, but under daylight conditions with fast prime lenses, this may be inconsequential. For example, an expedition photographer could probably cover most situations with a 28 mm *f*2.8 and a 100 mm *f*2.8 lens if he had a 2 and 3 times converter. This would give 28 mm *f*2.8, 56 mm *f*5.6, 84 mm *f*8, 100 mm *f*2.8, 200 mm *f*5.6 and 300 mm *f*8 combinations; not particularly impressive until you remember that with one lens on the camera the rest will go in one pocket. If absolute definition is of the utmost concern, however, the prime lenses and the converter must be of the highest quality. Unfortunately, even so, definition with converters, especially with wide-angle lenses is often well below optimum.

Zoom lenses allow you to cover a range of focal lengths, but their sizes, weights and maximum apertures are governed by their longest focal length. Thus an 85–200 mm lens is a versatile substitute for a 200 mm lens, but a clumsy one for an 85 mm. If you expect to use all the range quite often, a zoom lens may be a good addition to your system. If, however, most of your work is at one end or other, you would probably be better served by a suitable prime lens—and possibly a teleconverter for the odd occasion. Both these accessories are covered in more detail in other sections of this book.

Close-ups and special accessories

Close up equipment ranges from simple accessory lenses to microscopes. While accessory lenses are useful for the occasional job a set of extension tubes will give more versatility. To increase this further a set of extension bellows is useful but we are coming to equipment which needs a bag of its own, and if portability is the prime concern, the choice requires careful thought. Remember that it is difficult to use the full capabilities of even small bellows without a firm tripod or similar support. For many field shots, a longish lens (say 85–125 mm) with a small extension tube gives adequate image size without being a burden.

SLR cameras are simple to use on microscopes, usually with adapters supplied. However, photography is normally considered as an extension of microscopy, rather than vice versa, and a microscope would not normally be considered part of a camera system. Likewise, many astronomers—amateur and professional—use a camera with their telescopes, but the latter could not really be thought of as camera accessories.

Filters

Many photographers keep an ultra-violet absorbing filter permanently on their lenses to prevent damage. This is normally unnecessary except under hazardous conditions, and unless the filter is of superb quality, will probably reduce the absolute definition of negatives. Other filters should be considered as the occasion arises. If your lens set needs several different sizes, you may be able to economise by buying large filters and adapter rings.

Cases

Cases fall into two categories—ever-ready camera cases, lens cases etc. usually supplied by the equipment manufacturer, and gadget bags or equipment cases.

Ever-ready cases are a matter of taste—many photographers find them a nuisance, and often the best compromise is to remove the front flap and leave it at home, thus retaining some protection without inconvenience. They are, however, good for protecting the camera in storage, as are the round zip or clip up lens cases supplied with most lenses.

However, if you want to carry several items with you, the simplest way is to put them all into one case. If you carry the camera separately, a small gadget bag is very handy. The sort that are supposed to hold a camera and two accessory lenses will hold about three lenses, a small flashgun and several cassettes of film, together with filters, extension leads and other small items. For real strength, however, there is no substitute for foam-lined aluminium cases. These can be bought in a number of sizes, and have foam inserts which are cut to provide tight-fitting compartments for all your pieces of equipment. Professional photographers, who are not unduly worried about the looks of their equipment, tend to carry it loose in a leather hold-all. Whatever form your system case takes, you should leave all the individual cases behind—they take up space and get in the way. Lenses are quite safe with caps on both ends if they are kept in small polythene bags to prevent surface markings.

Fujica ST605

The Fujica ST605 is a 35 mm single lens reflex camera with a through the lens (TTL) exposure meter coupled with the shutter speed and the lens aperture. As you set aperture or shutter speed a needle moves across a scale in the viewfinder to indicate whether the controls are set for correct exposure or how much over- or under-exposure to expect. The meter switch causes the lens diaphragm to open and close as its control is operated, thus providing metering at the shooting aperture – stopped-down metering.

The camera uses 35 mm perforated film in standard cassettes to give pictures 36 x 24 mm. The shutter is a cloth focal plane type with speeds from 1/2 second to 1/700 second and a B setting for time exposures. It is synchronised for use with electronic flash at 1/60 second and slower or bulbs at 1/15 second or slower, with either cordless units via the contact in the accessory shoe (hot shoe) or with cord units connected to the coaxial socket on the camera front. A self-timer gives a delay of about 10 seconds that can be varied down to about 5 seconds.

The standard lens is the Fujinon 55 mm *f*2.2 with automatic diaphragm and focusing from 0.6 m (2 ft) to infinity.

The pentaprism eye-level viewfinder gives an almost life-size image with the 55 mm lens. It shows about 92 per cent of the image area that will appear on the film.

Exposure metering is by two silicon sensors, one on each side of the viewfinder eyepiece, giving an average reading of the whole viewfinder area. The meter works with any lens or accessory that can be connected to the camera. It has a film speed range from 25–3200 ASA and a capability of EV2 to EV17 with an *f*1.4 lens and 100 ASA film.

The film transport lever is of the single-stroke type with a hinged plastic tip to provide stand-off if required. Rewind is by orthodox crank and film release button. The frame counter shows the number of pictures taken and resets automatically when the camera back is opened.

With standard lens, the camera measures 133 x 86 x 88 mm ($5\frac{1}{4}$ x $3\frac{1}{8}$ x $3\frac{1}{2}$ in) and weighs 730 g (1lb 10oz). The camera body alone weighs 565 g (1lb 4oz).

Fujica ST605 features

1 Frame counter. **2** Shutter release. **3** Transport lever. **4** Film speed setting. **5** Shutter speed setting. **6** Viewfinder eyepiece. **7** Flash contact. **8** Focal plane mark. **9** Battery compartment. **10** Rewind crank. **11** Rewind knob. **13** Depth of field scale. **14** Focusing ring. **15** Distance scale. **16** Aperture setting. **17** Meter switch. **18** Self timer. **19** Rewind button. **20** Tripod socket. **21** Flash socket.

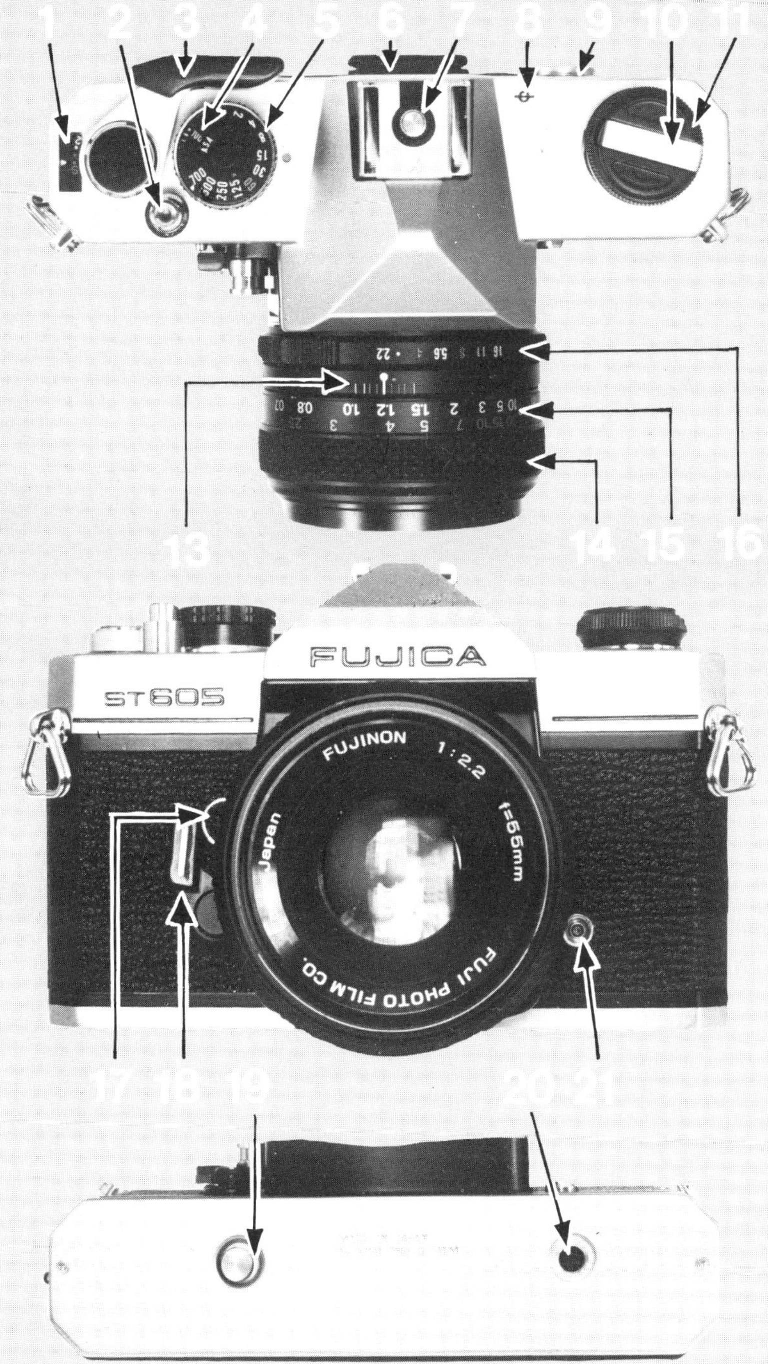
1 2 3 4 5 6 7 8 9 10 11
13 14 15 16
FUJICA
ST605
FUJINON 1:2.2
f=55mm
Japan
FUJI PHOTO FILM CO.
17 18 19 20 21

Fujica ST605

The Fujica ST605 exposure meter is powered by two silver oxide batteries housed in the back of the camera top plate. The operating switch is on the camera front and also acts as a stop-down button for depth of field preview. It is sprung to return to the full-aperture position when pressure is removed. It does not lock in the stop-down position.

The rectangular viewfinder eyepiece gives a clear image of the whole screen, even for most spectacle wearers. The screen has a fine-ground surface without fresnel rings. In the centre, a small split-image rangefinder section is surrounded by a microprism collar for focusing objects without straight lines. Around that is a very fine-ground area for critical focusing.

The meter readout is on the right of the screen. The meter needle should be centred in the cut-out to indicate correct exposure. Plus and minus signs indicate the tendency to over or under-exposure when aperture and shutter speed controls are wrongly set.

The back of the camera is hinged at the right and is opened by pulling the rewind knob upward. The take-up spool is multi-slotted to take the film leader.

In the camera baseplate are a tripod socket at the rewind end of the camera and a large film release button for rewinding.

Fujica ST605 features

1 Distance scale. **2** Focusing ring. **3** Meter switch. **4** Self timer. **5** Aperture setting. **6** Flash socket. **7** Viewfinder screen. **8** Fine-ground area. **9** Microprism. **10** Split-image rangefinder. **11** Overexposure warning. **12** Meter needle. **13** Underexposure warning.

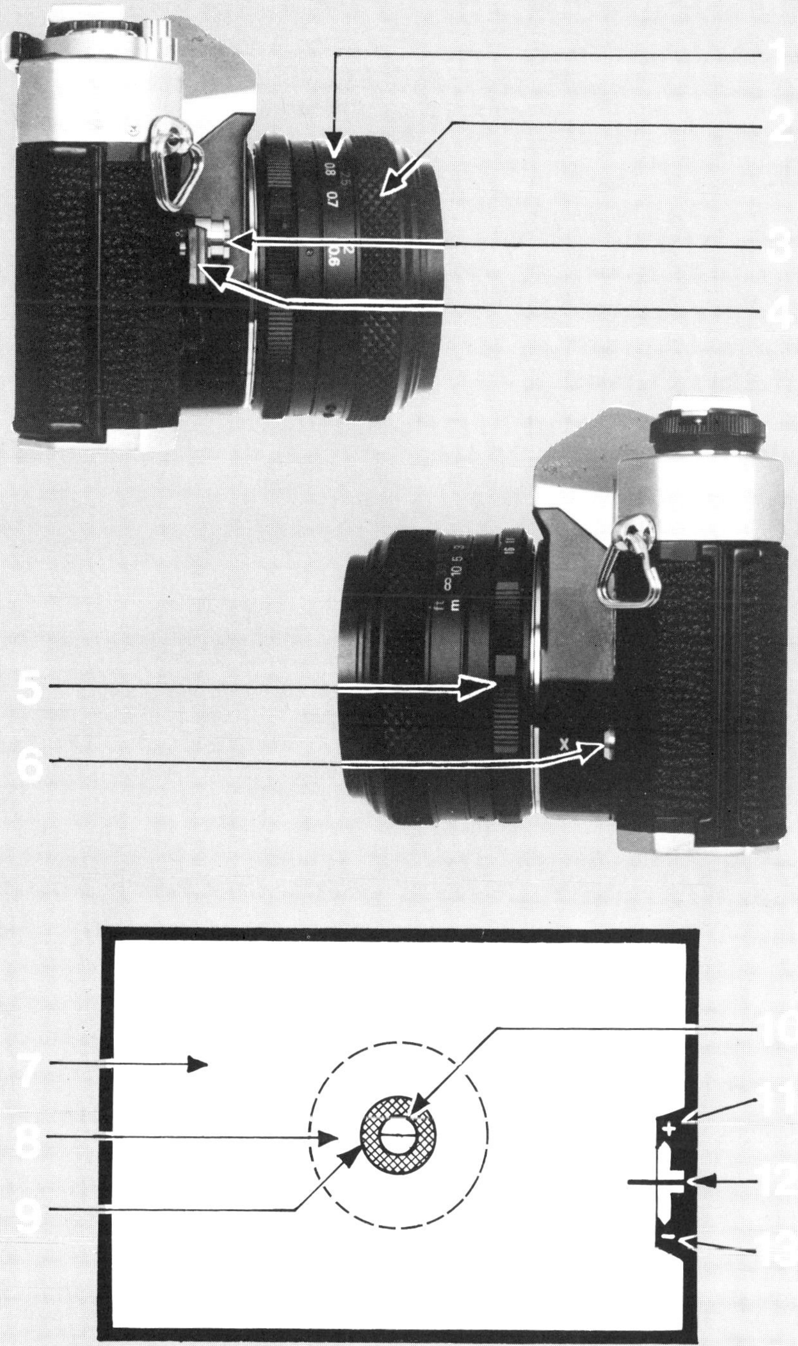
1
2
3
4
5
6
x
7
8
9
10
11
12
13
+
−

Fujica ST705

The Fujica ST705 is a 35 mm single lens reflex camera with a through-the-lens (TTL) exposure meter coupled with the shutter speed and lens aperture. As you set aperture or shutter speed a needle moves across a scale in the viewfinder to indicate whether the controls are set for correct exposure. The meter switch is incorporated in the shutter release, bringing the meter circuit into operation at the first light pressure. Accordingly the shutter release can be locked. The meter operates at full aperture with the appropriate Fujinon lenses and can also be used for stopped-down metering.

The camera uses 35 mm perforated film in standard cassettes to give pictures 36 x 24 mm. The shutter is a cloth focal-plane type with speeds from 1 second to 1/1500 second and a B setting for time exposures. It is synchronised for use with electronic flash at 1/60 second and slower or with M-class bulbs at 1/15 second and slower. Cordless units are connected via the contact in the accessory shoe (hot shoe), while units with synchronising cords are connected to the socket marked X on the camera front. Special "focal plane" bulbs can be used at shutter speeds of 1/60 second and faster in a unit connected to the socket marked FP on the camera front. A self-timer gives a delay of about 10 seconds, variable down to about 5 seconds.

The standard lens is either the Fujinon 50 mm *f*1.4 or the Fujinon 55 mm *f*1.8, with automatic diaphragm and focusing from 0.45 m (1ft 6in) to infinity.

Exposure metering is by two silicon sensors, one on each side of the viewfinder eyepiece, giving an average reading of the whole viewfinder area. The meter works with any lens or accessory that can be connected to the camera. It has a film speed range of 25–3200 ASA and a capability of EV1 to EV18.5 with *f*1.4 lens and 100 ASA film.

The film transport lever is of the single-stroke type with a hinged plastic tip to provide stand-off if required. Rewind is by orthodox crank and film release button. The frame counter shows the number of pictures taken and resets automatically when the camera back is opened.

With the *f*1.8 lens the camera measures 133 x 86 x 88 mm ($5\frac{1}{4}$ x $3\frac{1}{8}$ x $3\frac{1}{2}$ in) and weighs 780 g (1lb $11\frac{1}{2}$oz). The camera body alone weighs 580 g (1lb $4\frac{1}{2}$oz).

Fujica ST705 features

1 Frame counter. **2** Transport lever. **3** Film speed setting. **4** Shutter speed setting. **5** Flash contact. **6** Viewfinder eyepiece. **7** Accessory shoe. **8** Focal plane mark. **9** Battery compartment. **10** Rewind crank. **11** Shutter release. **12** Aperture setting. **13** Focusing ring. **14** Distance scale. **15** Depth of field scale. **16** Stop-down button. **17** Self timer. **18** Rewind button. **19** Tripod socket. **20** Flash socket (X). **21** Flash socket (FP)

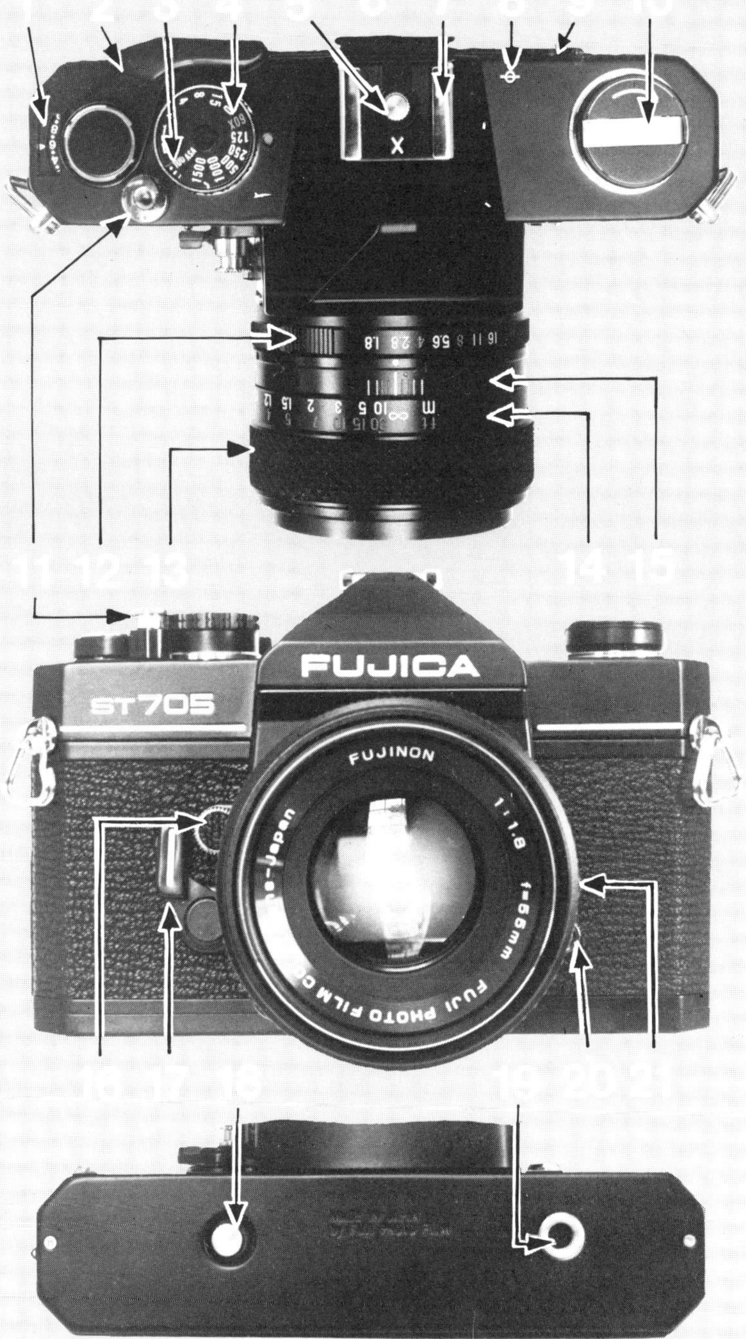
1
2
3
4
5
6
7
8
9
10
11
12
13
14
15
16
17
18
19
20
21
FUJICA
ST705
FUJINON
FUJI PHOTO FILM CO

Fujica ST705

The Fujica ST705 exposure meter is powered by two silver oxide batteries housed in the back of the camera top plate. It is operated by the first pressure on the shutter release button. A depth of field preview button next to the lens stops down the diaphragm to the pre-set aperture when pressed inward. It can be locked down for stopped-down metering.

The rectangular viewfinder eyepiece gives a clear image of the whole screen, even for most spectacle wearers. The screen has a fine-ground surface without fresnel rings. In the centre, a small split-image rangefinder section is surrounded by a microprism collar for focusing objects without straight lines. Around that is a very fine-ground area for critical focusing.

The meter readout is on the right of the screen. The meter needle should be centred in the cutout to indicate correct exposure. Plus and minus signs indicate the tendency to over- or under-exposure when aperture and shutter speed controls are wrongly set.

The back of the camera is hinged on the right and is opened by pulling the rewind knob upward. The take-up spool is multi-slotted to take the film leader.

In the camera baseplate are a tripod socket at the rewind end of the camera and a large film release button for rewinding.

Fujica ST705 features

1 Distance scale. **2** Focusing ring. **3** Stop-down button. **4** Lens lock release. **5** Aperture setting. **6** Flash socket (FP). **7** Flash socket (X). **8** Viewfinder screen. **9** Fine-ground area. **10** Microprism. **11** Split-image rangefinder. **12** Overexposure warning. **13** Meter needle. **14** Underexposure warning.

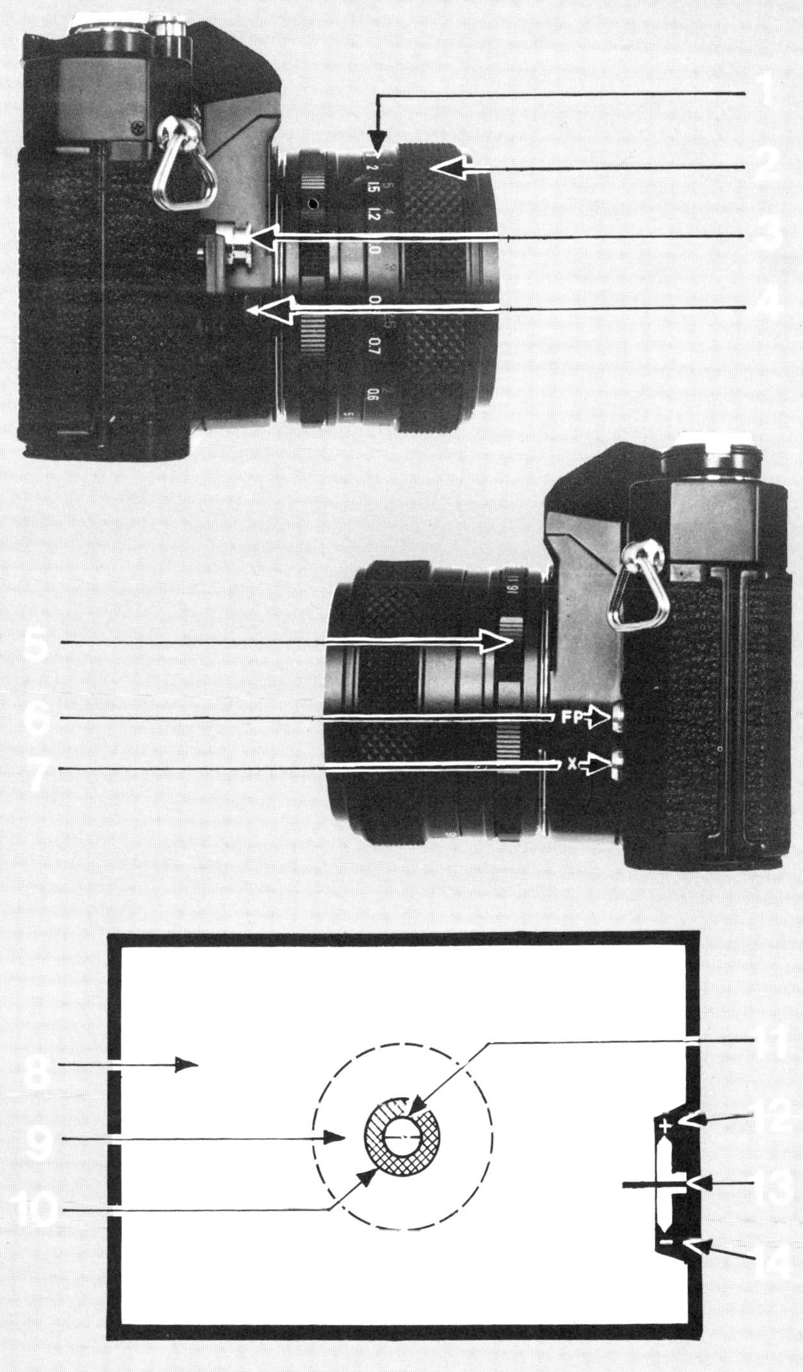
1
2
3
4
5
6
FP
7
X
8
9
10
11
12
+
13
14
−

Fujica ST801

The Fujica ST801 is a 35 mm single lens reflex camera with a through-the-lens (TTL) exposure meter coupled with the shutter speed and lens aperture. As you set aperture or shutter speed, light-emitting diodes (LEDs) glow in one or two of seven positions on a scale indicating correct and over- or under-exposure. The meter switch is incorporated in the shutter release, which can accordingly be locked. The meter operates at full aperture with the appropriate Fujinon lenses and can also be used for stopped-down metering.

The camera uses 35 mm perforated film in standard cassettes to give pictures 36 x 24 mm. The shutter is a cloth focal plane type with speeds from 1 second to 1/2000 second and a B setting for time exposures. It is synchronised for use with electronic flash at 1/60 second and slower or with M-class bulbs at 1/15 second and slower. Cordless units are connected via the contact in the accessory shoe (hot shoe), while units with synchronising cords are connected to the socket marked X on the camera front. Special "focal plane" bulbs can be used at shutter speeds of 1/60 second and faster in a unit connected to the socket marked FP on the camera front. A self-timer gives a delay of about 10 seconds, variable down to about 5 seconds.

The standard lens is either the Fujinon 50 mm *f*1.4 or the Fujinon 55 mm *f*1.8, with automatic diaphragm and focusing from 0.45 m (1ft 6in) to infinity.

Exposure metering is by two silicon sensors, one on each side of the viewfinder eyepiece, giving an average reading of the whole viewfinder area. The meter works with any lens or accessory that can be connected to the camera. It has a film speed range of 25–3200 ASA and a capability of EV1 to EV19 with *f*1.4 lens and 100ASA film.

The film transport lever is of the single-stroke type with a hinged plastic tip to provide stand-off if required. Rewind is by orthodox crank and film release button. The frame counter shows the number of pictures taken and resets automatically when the camera back is opened.

With the *f*1.8 lens, the camera measures 133 x 91 x 88 mm ($5\frac{1}{4}$ x $3\frac{7}{8}$ x $3\frac{1}{2}$ in) and weighs 830 g (1lb 13 oz). The camera body alone weighs 635 g (1lb $6\frac{1}{4}$ oz).

Fujica ST801 features

1 Frame counter. **2** Transport lever. **3** Shutter release. **4** Film speed setting. **5** Shutter speed setting. **6** Viewfinder eyepiece. **7** Flash contact. **8** Focal plane mark. **9** Battery compartment. **10** Rewind crank. **11** Rewind knob. **12** Aperture setting. **13** Distance scale. **14** Focusing ring. **15** Depth of field scale. **17** Carrying strap lug. **18** Self timer. **19** Stop-down button. **20** Lens. **21** Flash socket (FP). **22** Flash socket (X). **23** Rewind button. **24** Tripod socket.

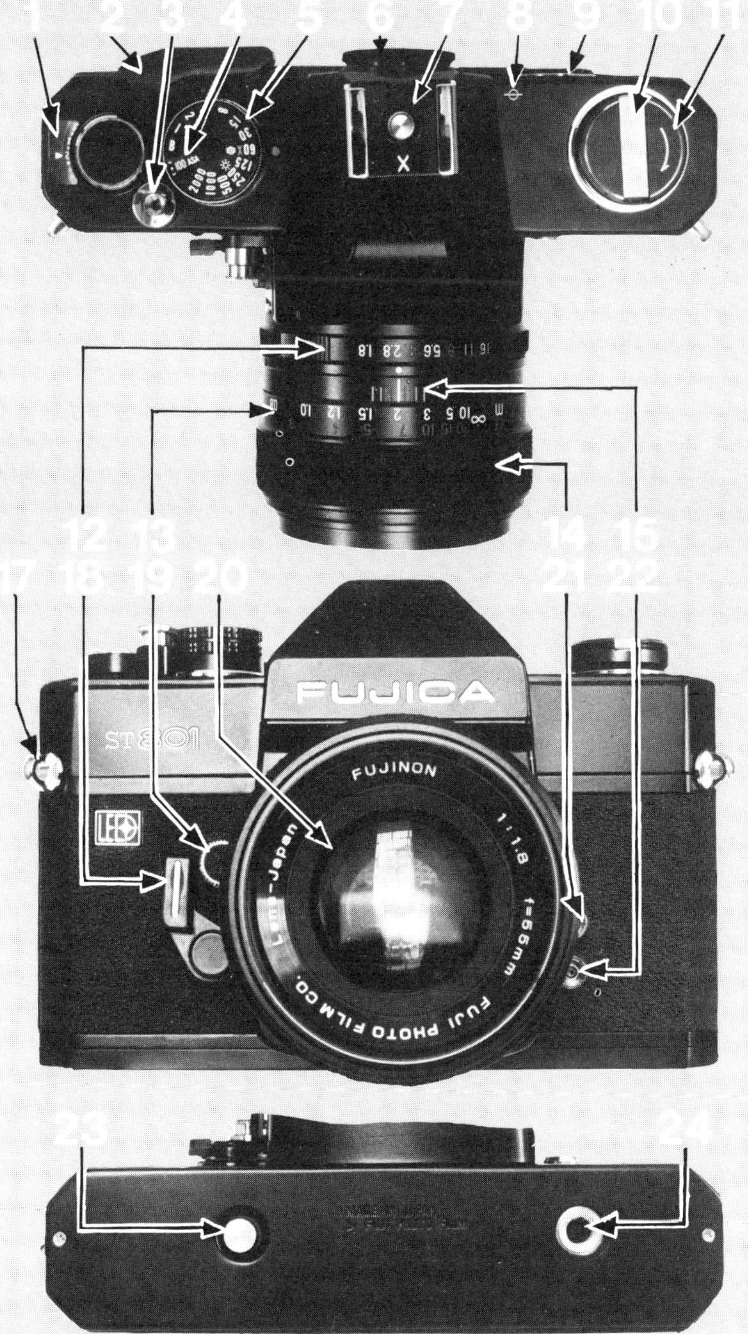

1
2
3
4
5
6
7
8
9
10
11
12
13
14
15
17
18
19
20
21
22
23
24
FUJICA
ST801
FUJINON
1:1.8 f=55mm
Lens-Japan
FUJI PHOTO FILM CO.

Fujica ST801

The Fujica ST801 exposure meter is powered by a single 6V silver oxide or manganese alkaline battery housed in the back of the camera top plate. It is operated by the first pressure on the shutter release button. A depth of field preview button next to the lens stops down the diaphragm to the preset aperture when pressed inward. It can be locked down for stopped-down metering.

The circular viewfinder eyepiece may tend to obscure the edges of the screen for some spectacle wearers. The screen has a fine-ground surface without fresnel rings. In the centre, a small split-image rangefinder section is surrounded by a microprism collar for focusing objects without straight lines. Around that is a very fine-ground area for critical focusing.

The meter readout is on the right of the screen. The centre, diamond-shaped LED should glow for correct exposure settings. The plus and minus signs indicate the tendency to over- or under-exposure when aperture and shutter speed controls are wrongly set.

The back of the camera is hinged on the right and is opened by pulling the rewind knob upward. The take-up spool is multi-slotted to take the film leader.

In the camera baseplate are a tripod socket at the rewind end of the camera and a large film release button for rewinding.

Fujica ST801 features

1 Carrying strap lug. **2** Distance scale. **3** Focusing ring. **4** Stop-down button. **5** Lens lock release. **6** Aperture setting. **7** Flash socket (FP). **8** Flash socket (X). **9** Split-image rangefinder. **10** Shutter speed. **11** Microprism. **12** Exposure indicator. **13** Light-emitting diodes. **14** Viewfinder screen.

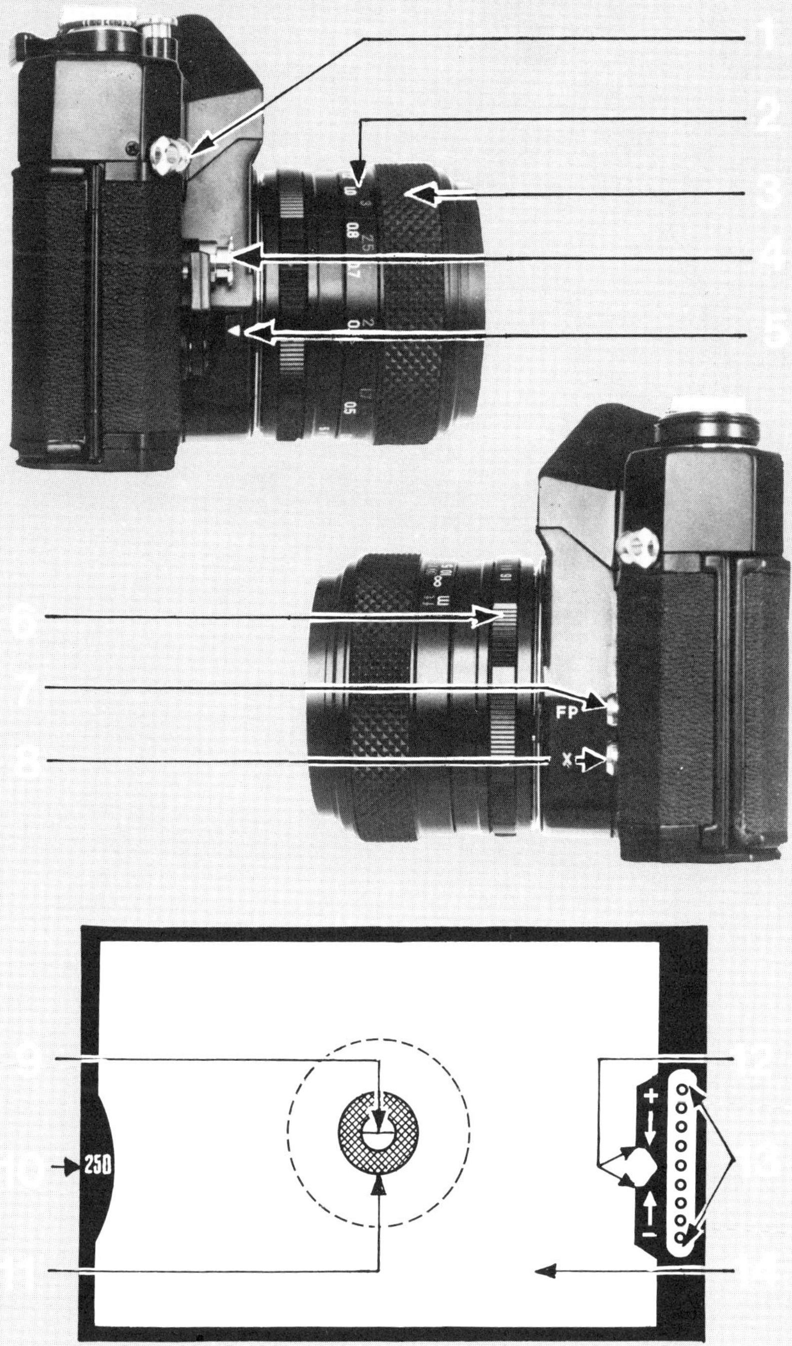
1
2
3
4
5
6
7
FP
8
X
9
10
250
11
12
+
–
13
14

Fujica ST901

The Fujica ST901 is an automatic exposure 35 mm single lens reflex camera with a through-the-lens (TTL) exposure meter coupled with the shutter speed and lens aperture. For automatic operation, you set the aperture and the meter circuit sets the shutter speed (aperture-preferred system) and provides a digital readout in the viewfinder. The camera can be operated manually (i.e. without meter) with a limited range of shutter speeds. The meter switch is incorporated in the shutter release, bringing the meter circuit into operation on the first light pressure. Accordingly, the shutter release can be locked. The meter operates at full aperture with the appropriate Fujinon lenses and can also be operated automatically in the stopped-down mode.

The camera uses 35 mm perforated film in standard cassettes to give pictures 36 x 24 mm. The shutter is a cloth focal plane type with marked manual speeds from 1/60 second to 1/1000 second and electronically-controlled automatic speeds continuously variable between 20 seconds and 1/1000 second. There is also a B setting for time exposures and a self-timer giving delays from 5 to 10 seconds on automatic or manual operation. A fractional exposure control is provided to influence the meter setting toward over- or under-exposure.

The shutter is synchronised for use with electronic flash at 1/60 second and B (manual operation) or when speeds of 20 seconds to 1/30 second are indicated on auto setting. There is a contact for cordless units in the accessory shoe (hot shoe) and a socket (marked X) on the camera front for cord units. Focal plane bulbs can be used with the manual shutter speeds in a unit connected to the FP socket. The camera is not designed for use with M or MF class bulbs.

The standard lens is either the Fujinon 50 mm *f*1.4 or the Fujinon 55 mm *f*1.8, with automatic diaphragm and focusing from 0.45 m (1 ft 6 in) to infinity.

Exposure metering is by two silicon sensors, one on each side of the viewfinder eyepiece, giving an average reading of the whole viewfinder area. The meter works with any lens or accessory that can be connected to the camera. It has a film speed range from 25 to 3200 ASA and a capability of EV–3 to EV18 with *f*1.4 lens and 100 ASA film.

The film transport lever is of the single-stroke type with a hinged plastic tip to provide stand-off if required. Rewind is by orthodox crank and film release button. The frame counter shows the number of pictures taken and resets automatically when the camera back is opened.

With the *f*1.8 lens, the camera measures 133 x 92 x 91 mm ($5\frac{1}{4}$ x $3\frac{5}{8}$ x $3\frac{5}{8}$ in) and weighs 830 g(1 lb 13 oz). The camera body alone weighs 630 g (1 lb 6 oz).

Fujica ST901 features

1 Frame counter. **2** Transport lever. **3** Shutter release. **4** Shutter speed setting. **5** Auto setting. **6** Viewfinder eyepiece. **7** Flash contact. **8** Eyepiece shutter control. **9** Battery compartment. **10** Focal plane mark. **11** Rewind crank. **12** Shutter release lock. **13** Film speed setting. **14** Auto/manual lever. **15** Aperture setting. **16** Focusing ring. **17** Distance scale. **18** Depth of field scale. **19** Depth of field preview. **20** Self timer. **21** Rewind button. **22** Lens. **23** Tripod socket. **24** Flash socket (X). **25** Flash socket (FP).

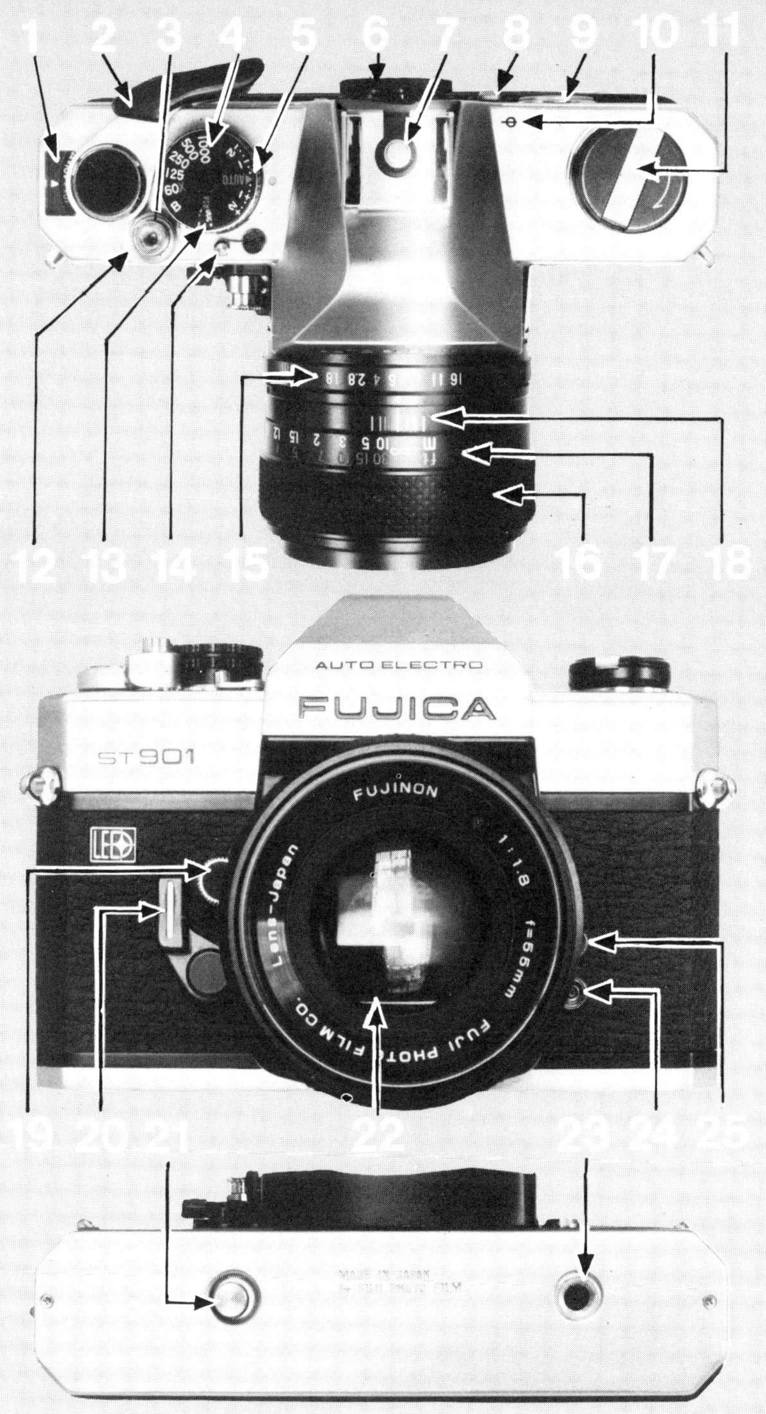

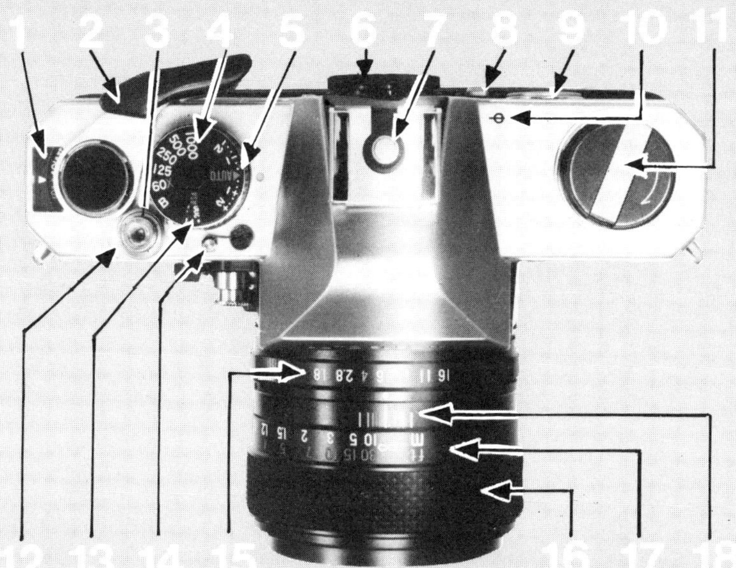
1 2 3 4 5 6 7 8 9 10 11
1000 500 250 125 60 B
AUTO
16 11 4 2.8 1.8
12 13 14 15 16 17 18

AUTO ELECTRO
FUJICA
ST901
FUJINON
1:1.8 f=55mm
FUJI PHOTO FILM CO.
Lens-Japan
19 20 21 22 23 24 25
MADE IN JAPAN
by FUJI PHOTO FILM

Fujica ST901

The Fujica ST901 exposure meter is powered by a single 6V silver oxide or manganese alkaline battery housed in the back of the camera top plate. It is operated by the first pressure on the shutter release button. A depth of field preview button next to the lens stops down the lens to its preset aperture when turned and pressed inward. It can be locked down for stopped-down metering.

The circular viewfinder eyepiece may tend to obscure the edges of the screen for some spectacle wearers. It is fitted with a shutter to protect the meter sensors from extraneous light when the camera is used for long exposures unattended. The screen has a fine-ground surface without fresnel rings. In the centre, a small split-image rangefinder section is surrounded by a microprism collar for focusing objects without straight lines. Around that is a very fine ground area for critical focusing.

The meter readout is a digital indication of the shutter speed appearing above the viewfinder. It operates only with the shutter speed knob set to AUTO.

The back of the camera is hinged on the right and is opened by pulling the rewind knob upward. The take-up spool is multi-slotted to accept the film leader. A peep window in the back allows you to see the cassette in the film chamber to remind you which Fuji film you have loaded.

In the camera baseplate are a tripod socket at the rewind end of the camera and a large film release button for rewinding.

Fujica ST901 features

1 Distance scale. **2** Focusing ring. **3** Depth of field preview. **4** Lens lock release. **5** Aperture setting. **6** Flash socket (FP). **7** Flash socket (X). **8** Shutter speed. **9** Auto/manual signal. **10** Microprism. **11** Viewfinder screen. **12** Split-image rangefinder.

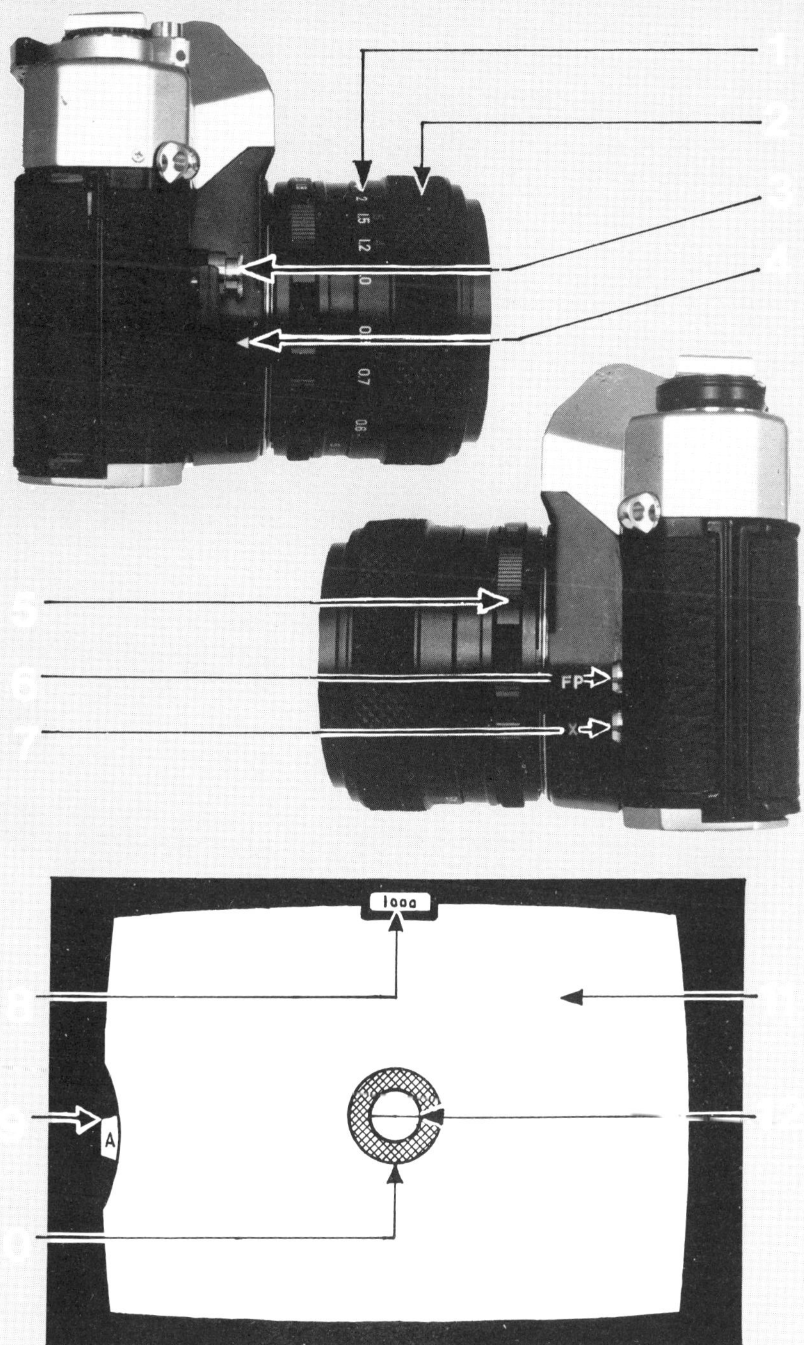

1
2
3
4
5
FP
6
X
7
1000
8
9
A
10

Fujica AZ-1

Like the ST901, the Fujica AZ-1 is an aperture-preferred automatic exposure model with TTL meter coupled with shutter speed and lens aperture. There are, however, significant differences in design and operation, mainly in the shutter.

For automatic operation, you set the aperture and the shutter speed is set by the meter circuit and indicated by LEDs on a scale in the viewfinder. The camera can be operated manually (without meter) with a limited range of shutter speeds. The meter switch is incorporated in the shutter release, bringing the meter circuit into operation on the first light pressure. While the pressure is maintained, the reading is locked, irrespective of changes in camera settings or light intensity. The meter operates at full aperture with the appropriate Fujinon lenses and can also operate automatically in the stopped-down mode.

The camera uses 35 mm perforated film in standard cassettes to give pictures 36 x 24 mm. The shutter is a cloth focal plane type with marked manual speeds of 1/60, 1/250 and 1/1000 second and B. The self timer gives delays of about 5 to 10 seconds. A fractional exposure control is provided.

The shutter is synchronised for use with electronic flash at manual settings of 1/60 second and B or when the viewfinder readout indicates a shutter speed of 1/60 second or slower. A special auto-exposure flash unit is available. Bulb flash is synchronised when the viewfinder readout indicates 1/2 to 1/15 second shutter speed. Flash contacts are in the accessory shoe and on the camera front.

Exposure metering is by a single silicon sensor giving a centre-weighted average reading. The meter works with any lens or accessory that can be connected to the camera. It has a film speed range of 25–3200 ASA and a capability of EV2–18 with *f*1.4 lens and 100 ASA film.

The film transport lever is of the single stroke type with hinged plastic tip for stand-off if required. Rewind is by orthodox crank and film release button. The frame counter shows the number of pictures taken and resets automatically when the camera back is opened.

The camera body measures 133 x 87.5 x 50.5 mm ($5\frac{1}{4}$ x 3 3/16 x 2 in) and weighs 580 g (20.4 oz).

Fujica AZ–1 features

1 Frame counter. **2** Shutter release. **3** Shutter speed setting. **4** Transport lever. **5** Auto setting. **6** Viewfinder eyepiece. **7** Accessory shoe. **8** Focal plane mark. **9** Battery compartment. **10** Rewind crank. **11** Carrying strap lug. **12** Shutter release lock. **13** Film speed setting. **14** Self timer. **15** Depth of field preview. **16** Focusing ring. **17** Distance scale. **18** Depth of field scale. **19** Aperture setting. **20** Flash contact. **21** Lens.

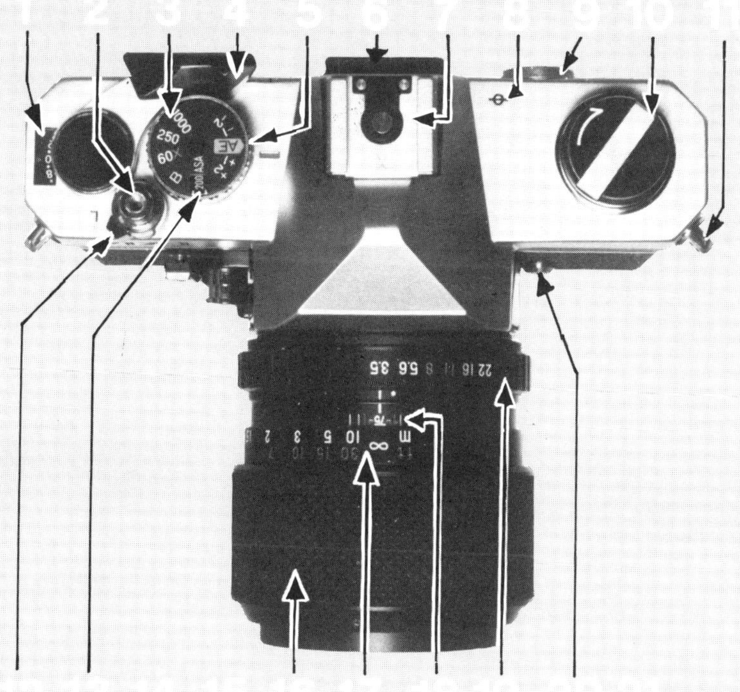
1 2 3 4 5 6 7 8 9 10 11
1000
250
60
B
AE
ASA
22 16 11 8 5.6 3.5
M
ft
∞ 30 15 10 7
10 5 3 2
12 13 14 15 16 17 18 19 20 21

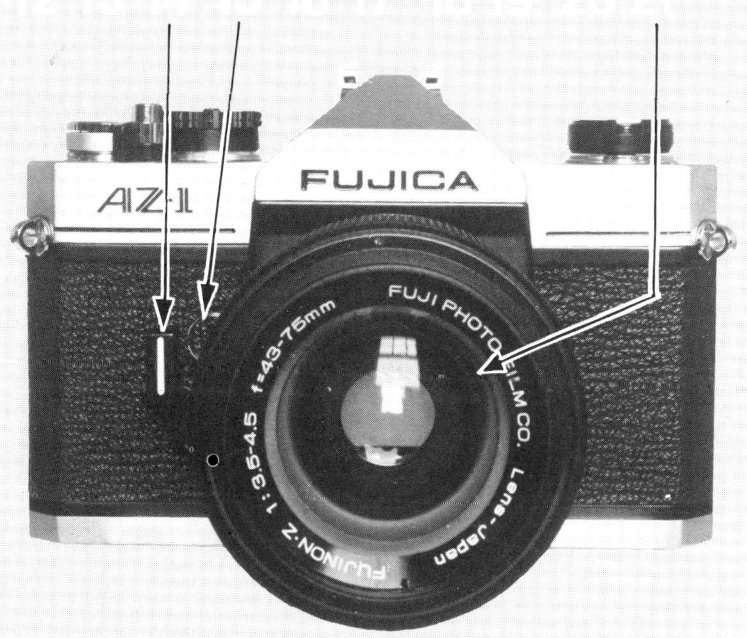
FUJICA
AZ-1
FUJI PHOTO FILM CO. Lens-Japan
FUJINON·Z 1:3.5-4.5 f=43-75mm

Fujica AZ-1

The Fujica AZ-1 exposure meter is powered by three 1.5 volt silver oxide batteries (Mallory MS76 or similar) housed in the back of the camera top plate. It is operated by first pressure on the shutter release button. A depth of field preview button next to the lens stops down the lens to the preset aperture when pressed inward.

The viewfinder eyepiece is rectangular, giving a clear view of the fine-ground screen with no fresnel lines. A small split-image rangefinder section in the centre is surrounded by a microprism collar and a further much larger very fine ground area for critical focusing.

The meter readout is a shutter speed scale with seven LEDs. It operates only with the shutter speed knob set to AE or to one of the exposure compensation figures (–2, –1, +1 or +2).

The back of the camera is hinged at the right and is opened by pulling the rewind knob upward. The take-up spool is multi-slotted to accept the film leader.

In the camera baseplate are a tripod socket at the rewind end of the camera and a large rewind button, as well as the special features of the AZ-1 – the motor coupling gear and electrical contacts for the Fujica Auto Winder.

Fujica Auto Winder

Designed to transport the film and cock the shutter automatically after each exposure, the Fujica Auto Winder simply screws into the camera baseplate. Engage the slotted lug on the end of the Winder with the protruding stud at the end of the camera baseplate, line up the tripod screw with the camera tripod socket and screw it in. Switch on the Winder and you are ready for motorised shooting. Automatic winding on occurs when you let go of the shutter release.

The Winder takes four AA size batteries which are loaded in from one end after pushing upward on the battery compartment cover to remove it. This cover can be difficult to remove when certain types of battery are loaded (such as the Crompton Vidor alkali manganese, which are fractionally longer than the Mallory equivalents).

Overall measurements of the Winder are 134 x 43 x 36 mm ($5\frac{1}{4}$ x $1\frac{5}{8}$ x $1\frac{3}{8}$ in). It weighs about 385 g (13.6 oz).

Fujica AZ–1 features

1 Auto Winder gear. **2** Rewind button. **3** Tripod socket. **4** Auto Winder contacts. **5** Lens lock release. **6** Auto Winder latch. **7** Depth of field preview. **8** Viewfinder screen. **9** Fine-ground area. **10** Microprism. **11** Split-image rangefinder. **12** Shutter speeds. **13** Overexposure warning. **14** LED indicating shutter speed. **15** Slow speed and underexposure warning.

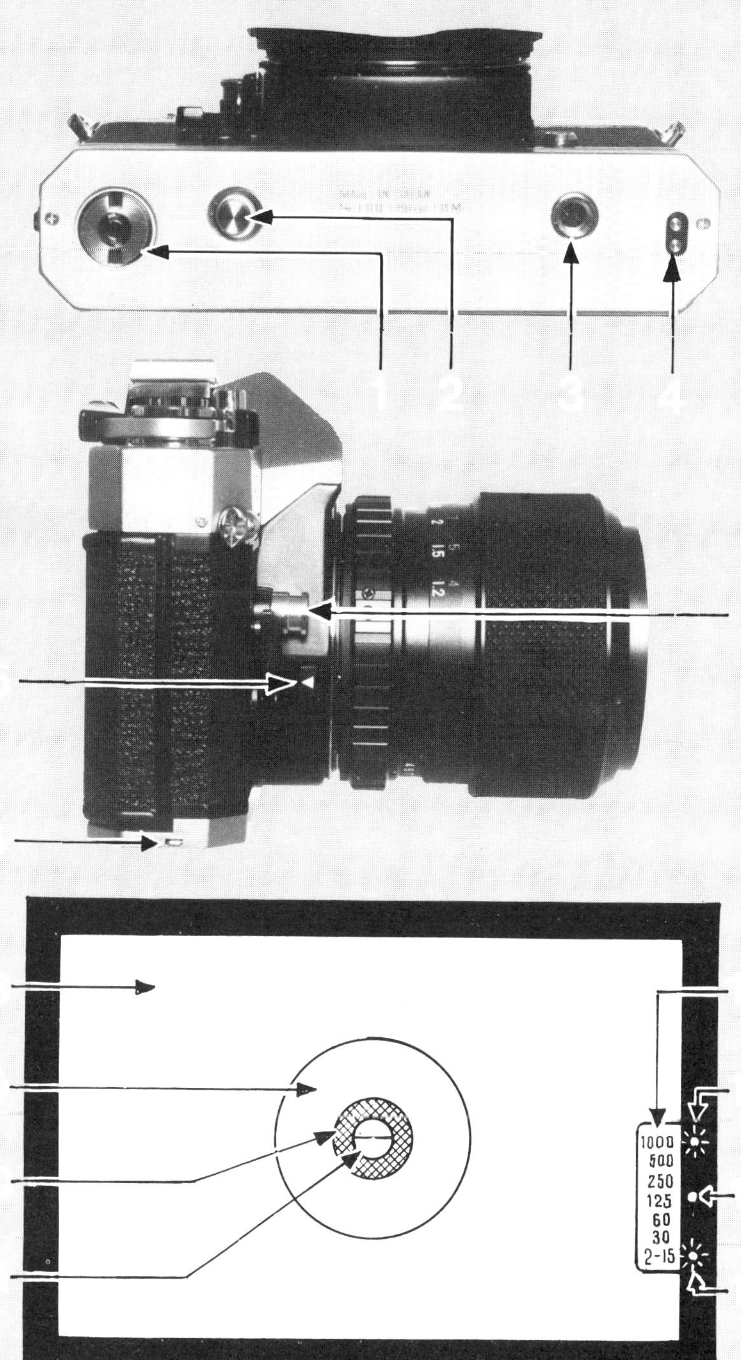

1
2
3
4
5
6
7
8
9
10
11
1000
500
250
125
60
30
2-15

Viewing and focusing

The Fujica viewfinder screen is a bright matt area with a central split-image rangefinder surrounded by a microprism collar and an outer fine-ground ring for critical focusing. Each of these areas is useful in various conditions. The split-image rangefinder is the fastest in use when the subject has well-defined straight lines. The microprism area is only fractionally slower and is better suited to textured subjects. The very fine ground area enables you to focus close-range subjects critically, especially at small apertures. The major part of the screen is rarely used for focusing except by those already accustomed to screen focusing.

Rangefinder focusing

The image that will appear on the film is projected on to the screen by the camera lens. In the central rangefinder spot, any vertical straight line in the image is displaced in the two halves of the spot. As you turn the lens focusing ring the lens moves backward or forward to focus on farther or nearer objects respectively. To focus on a particular object you turn the ring until the images in top and bottom half of the central spot join into a straight line. In the microprism area, the image is grainy and shimmering when unsharp but steadies and looks sharper as you bring it into focus. On the rest of the screen, the image simply looks unsharp when not properly focused.

The split-image and microprism sections are not efficient at apertures smaller than *f*4 and it is preferable to use the matt area in those conditions.

Full-aperture focusing

Generally speaking, focusing at full aperture is always preferable because depth of field (see page 37) is then least and the image moves quickly in and out of focus as the setting of the lens focusing ring is varied. As most of the lenses for the Fujica cameras have automatic diaphragms that do not stop down until the shutter release is pressed, focusing at full aperture is the normal procedure.

Image size and area

The image on the screen is almost life size with a 50 mm lens focused at infinity. With other lenses it varies directly with the focal length, being, for example, nearly eight times life size with a 400 mm lens. The area shown is slightly less than that which will appear on the film because most slide mounts and enlarger masking frames have apertures slightly smaller than the standard 35 mm frame size.

Viewfinder features

1 Microprism. **2** Viewfinder screen. **3** Split-image rangefinder.
As you turn the focusing ring to the subject distance the microprism area becomes sharp and clear; the displaced halves of the split-image rangefinder area become continuous.

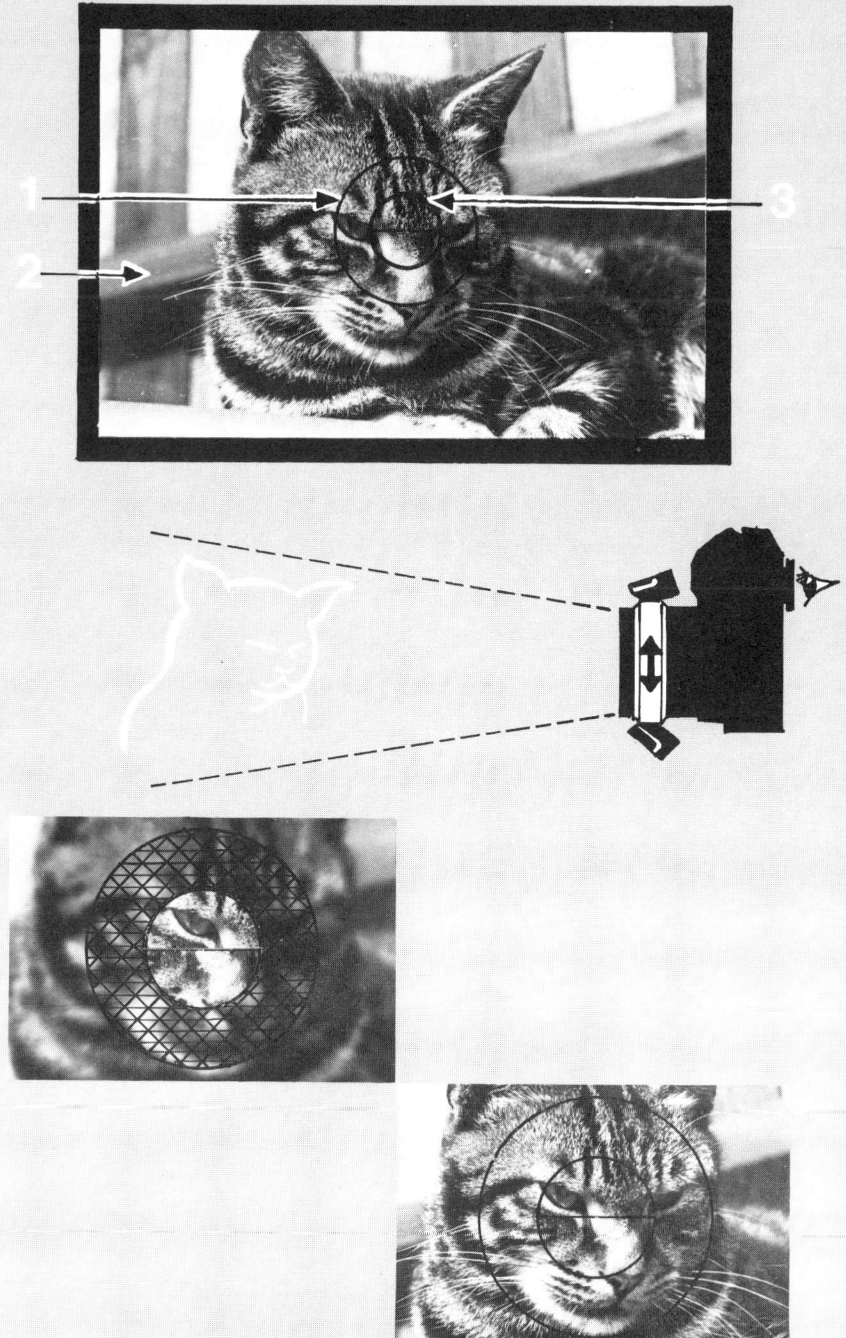
1
2
3

Focusing methods

One of the few camera operations that has not yet been satisfactorily automated is the task of adjusting the lens position to provide a sharp image on the film—known slightly inaccurately as focusing the lens. It is not always a simple operation.

When you have a single main subject or the whole of the subject is more or less in the same plane, there is no problem, but many subjects occupy some depth in space (as in landscapes) and the focus has to be placed with some care. When, for example, the landscape has the classic open gate in the foreground to lead the eye into the picture and out to the line of hills beyond, you do not focus on either the gate or the hills. You have to choose an aperture and focused distance to give you the depth of field required. If any sacrifice in sharpness is to be made it should usually be in the background rather than the foreground. A similar principle applies to almost any subject in depth. The usual advice is to focus at a point about one-third into the zone required to be sharp but it is generally easier to set the distance of your farthest required sharp plane to the "far" aperture number at which you are shooting on the depth of field scale (or preferably at one stop larger). Then check that the depth of field provided is adequate to cover the nearest required plane.

With reflex cameras you can, of course, check the screen image by using the depth of field preview button, but screen texture does tend to sharpen the image and at small apertures it is not easily seen.

Action and movement

Focusing a moving object can raise problems because the delay between focusing and shooting can result in the subject moving well out of focus again.

When the subject is moving within or can be confined to, a reasonably restricted area, the technique of zone focusing is useful. This makes use of depth of field again. You set your lens to the smallest practicable aperture and set the lens distance scale to a mid-point that allows the depth of field to cover the required zone. A football photographer, for example, might wish to cover action within the penalty area from behind the goal. If he focuses on 20 ft at *f* 8 with a 50 mm lens he will just about cover that zone. You can work out your own zones for your own purposes by consulting depth of field tables or the indicator on your lens.

Objects that move in a predictable direction, such as racing cars, athletes, etc., are more easily dealt with by focusing on a spot that the subject has to pass and releasing the shutter as the spot is reached. A sports or frame finder is a useful accessory for such shots to enable you to keep your eye on the subject before it reaches the selected spot.

Depth of field

In theory, a lens placed at a given distance from the image plane (the film) produces a sharp image of objects in a single plane at a certain distance in front of the lens. Objects in front of or behind that plane are rendered less sharply.

In practice, each image point formed by a lens is, in fact, a disc of finite size and, up to a certain degree of enlargement for a given viewing distance, the difference between the smallest possible disc and various slightly larger discs is indistinguishable to the human eye. The relative sizes of the various discs or image points formed by a lens can be envisaged by regarding the light reflected from the point and concentrated by the lens as a solid cone, with the effective aperture of the lens as its base. Thus, when the aperture is small and/or the lens-to-subject distance is large, the cone is relatively slender. At its apex (the crossover point for objects behind the focused plane), there is a relatively deep zone both fore and aft in which the discs formed by a section through the cone are still small enough to be rendered as discs indistinguishable from points on the film and, indeed, on considerably enlarged images.

This zone is the depth of field. As our explanation implies, it is greater when the effective lens aperture is smaller and when the focused distance is greater.

Enlargement and viewing distance

A complication arises with the comparatively small negative or slide sizes used today. Most final images, whether prints or projected slides, are considerably larger than the images produced on the film. Moreover, many prints are made from only part of the negative image and the degree of enlargement is not proportional to the print size. But most final images are viewed from a distance appropriate to their size, not, as they ideally should be, to their degree of enlargement. The complication then is that detail which looks sharp when enlarged less or viewed from a greater distance looks distinctly less sharp when enlarged to a greater degree or viewed from closer range.

Depth of field formulae and tables, therefore, must always be regarded as approximations. Although it is possible to make exact mathematical calculations based on focal length, *f*-number, focused distance and the size of the acceptable disc (known in this context as the circle of confusion), it is self-evident that you do not produce a sharp image of an object at 10.1 metres and an unsharp image of an object at 10.11 or even 10.2 metres. Depending on the use you wish to make of depth of field or the lack of it, you should always use at least a stop smaller or larger than calculators, indicators or tables recommend.

Changing the focused distance

In many cases, you can manipulate depth of field by changing your focused distance. When you want to throw the background out of focus, for example, you can focus forward a little, so that the subject is within the depth of field but the background is well behind it. The opposite also applies. If you focus slightly beyond the subject you extend the zone of sharpness behind it.

When you wish to obtain the greatest depth of field at any given aperture you set the focus at the hyperfocal distance for that aperture. This distance can be calculated or looked up in tables but the easiest method is to set the lens distance scale so that the infinity marking is opposite the *f*-number at which you are shooting on the depth of field scale. You are then focused at the hyperfocal distance and the depth of field stretches from half that distance to infinity.

Exposure controls

To obtain an image of a subject on film, you have to expose the film to the light rays reflected by that subject and focused on the film. The amount of light reaching the film varies with the amount of light reflected by the subject. That, in turn, varies with the strength of the light falling on the subject and the efficiency with which the subject reflects that light.

The film needs a certain amount of light to form a satisfactory image – the actual amount depending on the sensitivity or speed of the film. Thus, we need controls to match the light reflected from the subject to the sensitivity of the film. The camera allows us to use both time and intensity in this way (*top*).

To control the length of time for which the light is allowed to act on the film, we can vary the shutter speed.

To control the intensity of the light that is allowed to act on the film, we can obscure part of the lens by means of a variable aperture or stop.

Shutter operation

On the Fujica cameras the shutter can be set to give automatically-timed exposures varying with the model, or manually-controlled exposures of any duration by setting the shutter speed ring to B. The automatic speeds double up in the sequence.

2000 1000 500 250 125 60 30 15 8 4 2 1

These figures are the denominators of the appropriate fractions of a second, 125 denoting 1/125 second, etc.

Aperture settings

Similarly, the intensity of the light can be varied in doubling or halving steps by obscuring more or less of the lens rather in the manner of drawing curtains across a window (*bottom*). Camera lenses, however, have diaphragms consisting of metal leaves forming a continuously variable, more or less circular opening. The diaphragm is controlled by an aperture ring on the lens with click stops at specific, marked positions. These markings are in the sequence

1 1.4 2 2.8 4 5.6 8 11 16 22 32

and are known as *f*-numbers or relative apertures. For each lens, the ends of the scale vary, some stopping at *f*16 and perhaps starting at intermediate figures such as 1.8, 3.5, etc.

Exposure controls

Exposure is the product of time (shutter speed) and intensity (aperture). For a given film speed in given lighting conditions, there is one such product to provide correct exposure, but it can be obtained by various settings of the camera controls.

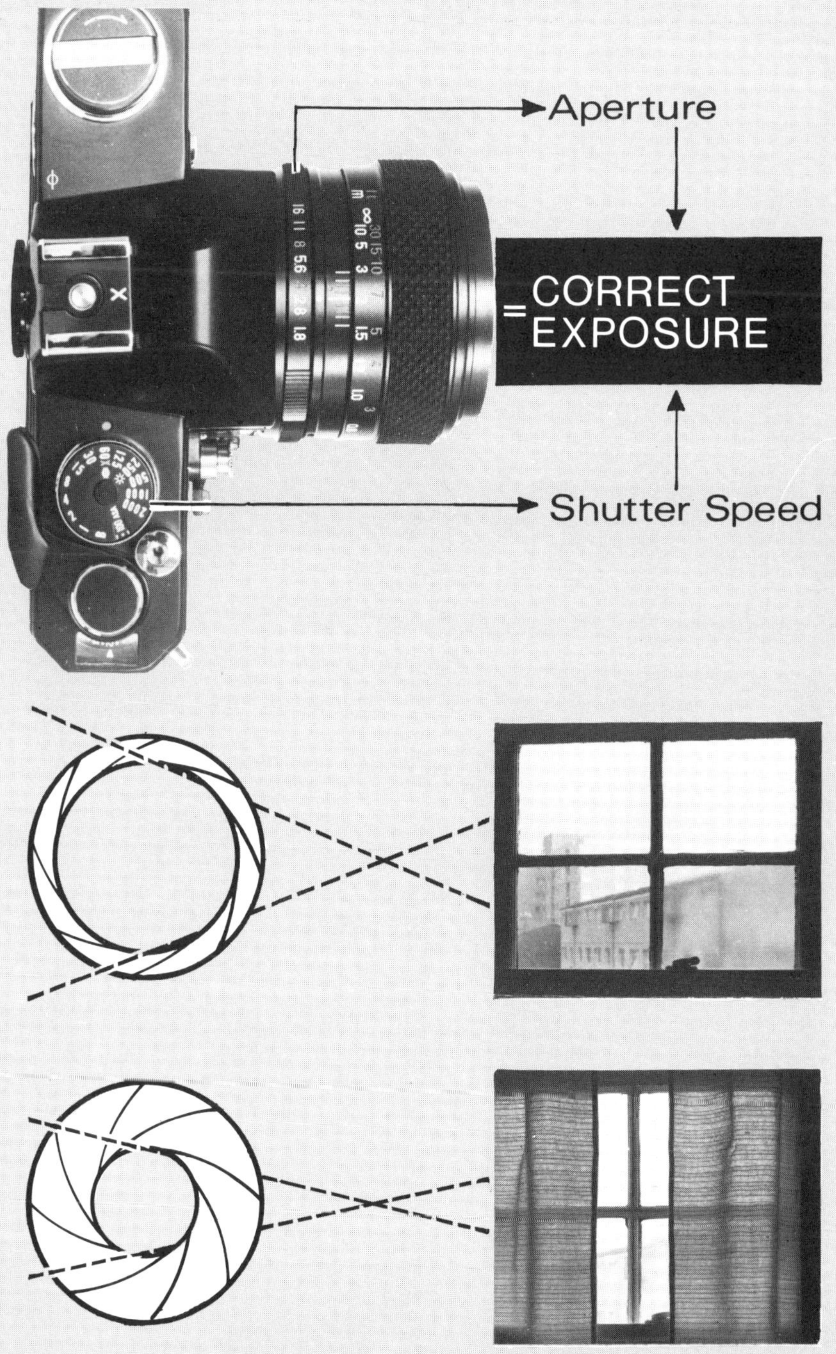
Aperture
=CORRECT EXPOSURE
Shutter Speed

Shutter operation

The shutter of the Fujica cameras is a focal plane type, which means that it is located within the camera body as close as possible to the film. It consists of two fabric blinds on rollers. When the shutter release is pressed, one blind moves across the film horizontally and is followed by the other at an interval depending on the shutter speed set. At the faster shutter speeds, the second blind follows the first very quickly, so that the film is, in effect, exposed strip by strip through the narrow gap between the two blinds. At slower speeds, the delay before the second blind is released is greater and the gap between the blinds is correspondingly larger. As the actual speed of traverse of the blinds remains constant, there comes a time when the gap has to be as wide as the image format. This, in fact, occurs at a shutter speed setting on the Fujicas of 1/60 second. At that and at all slower settings, the whole image is recorded simultaneously.

This type of shutter is very efficient but it has its drawbacks when you use flash equipment.

Setting the shutter speed

The shutter speed is set manually on the Fujicas by rotating the shutter speed knob until the appropriate figure is opposite the dot index to the left of the knob. Settings between the marked speeds cannot be used. On the Fujica ST901, the shutter speed is generally set automatically.

The shutter is tensioned automatically as you advance the film after each exposure and is opened by pressing the shutter release knob on the camera front or by cable release screwed into the centre of the knob.

The shutter speed you set depends on the nature of the subject and exposure requirements in conjunction with the aperture as determined by the exposure meter.

A static subject can be shot at any speed. A moving subject means blur if shot at a slow shutter speed. Really fast-moving subjects may call for speeds of 1/500 or 1/1000 second.

Delaying the shutter release

All the Fujica cameras have a delay mechanism allowing the shutter to be released several seconds after the delay is activated. First tension the shutter by transporting the film. Then pull the lever on the camera front below the shutter speed knob downward through an arc to the limit of its travel. Press the small button then revealed and the delay will start to run with an audible buzz. The shutter is released about 10 seconds after you press the button. You can shorten the delay to about five seconds by moving the lever only to about the horizontal position, but practise it with an empty camera first. If you should change your mind after activating the delay, you can release the shutter in the normal way and let the delay run down.

Shutter speed and subject

TOP
Providing the camera is adequately supported, a still life can be shot at a slow speed.
MIDDLE
Moving subjects need faster speeds. Even 1/60 sec is relatively slow when the subject is fast-moving. The picture is therefore blurred.
BOTTOM
To freeze fast movement, you need the fastest practicable speed.

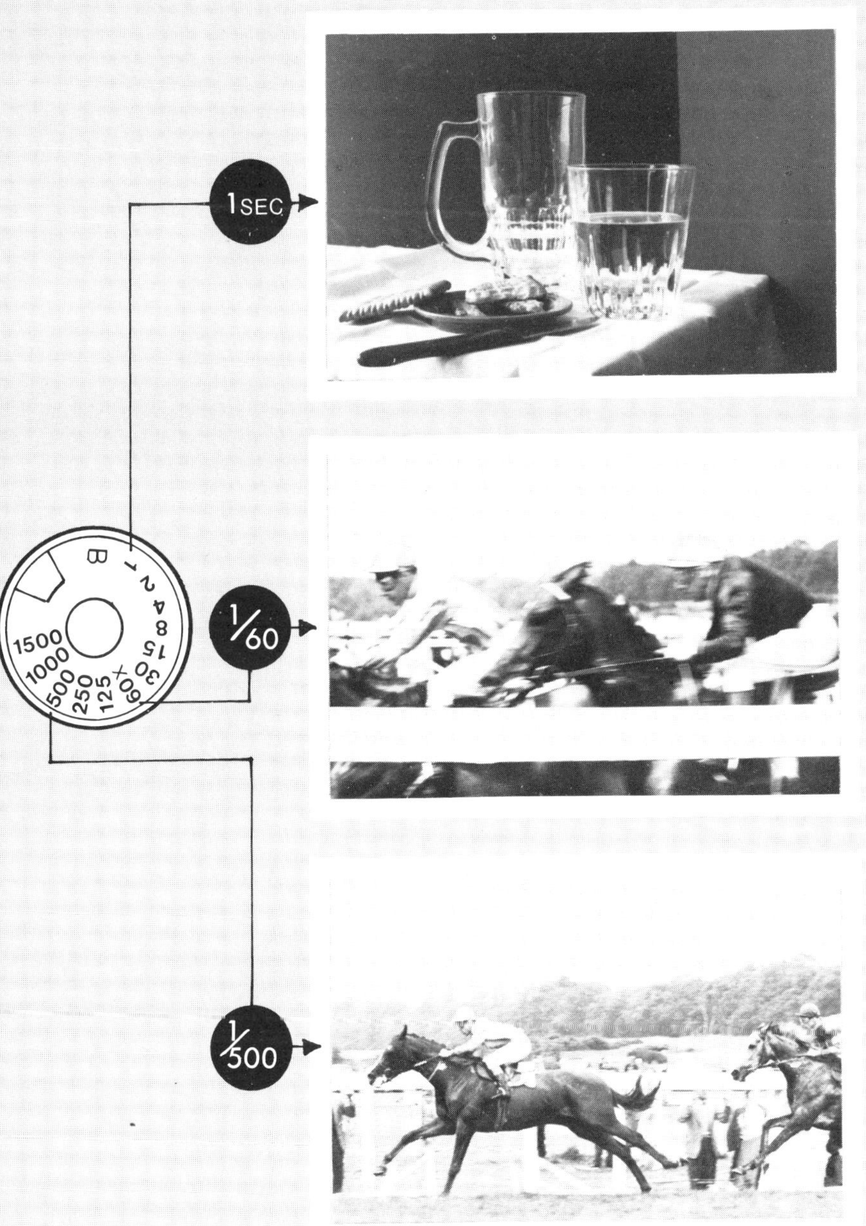
B
1
2
4
8
15
30
60 X
125
250
500
1000
1500
1 SEC
1/60
1/500

Exposure and exposure meters

Cameras have two controls over the amount of light that is allowed to act on the film—the shutter, with variable speeds controlling the time during which the light passes, and the aperture, a variable opening in a diaphragm which controls the intensity. Exposure is thus the product of time and intensity and the photographer's task is to choose a pair of settings which, taking into consideration the speed of the film and the lighting conditions, will produce a correctly exposed picture.

The simplest method of assessing the correct exposure is the rule of thumb which says that bright sunny lighting calls for an aperture of *f* 16 and the shutter speed numerically nearest to the film speed, i.e. 1/125 sec at *f* 16 for a 125 ASA film. For cloudy-bright lighting use *f* 11, overcast *f* 8, heavy cloud *f* 5.6 and dull *f* 4. So, in the overcast conditions an 80 ASA film would need 1/80 sec at *f* 8, which could be achieved with 1/60 at *f* 8 (or a fraction toward *f* 11).

The leaflet packed with the film gives sample exposures generally closely following this rule and if you use the exposures there given, you will not go far wrong. Naturally, you do not have to use the actual settings quoted. Either shutter speed or aperture can be adjusted to suit the subject. The 1/125 sec at *f* 16 we quoted could be altered to 1/500 sec at *f* 8 for a fast-moving subject. This is a shortening of time and increase of intensity that provides the same result.

Typical outdoor exposures—aperture at 1/500 sec.

	Film speeds ASA				
Weather Conditions	**25–40**	**50–80**	**100–160**	**200–320**	**400–640**
Bright sun* in bright surroundings	5.6	8	11	16	22
Bright or hazy sun	4	5.6	8	11	16
Light overcast	2.8	4	5.6	8	11
Cloudy	2	2.8	4	5.6	8
Dull**	1.4	2	2.8	4	5.6

*White sand, snow, whitewashed buildings, etc.
**Also subjects in the shade on sunny days.
Backlit subjects need about two stops more exposure in harsh lighting conditions.
One hour after sunrise, and one hour before sunset, give one stop more exposure.
In winter months give one stop more exposure.

How exposure meters work

Exposure meters are calibrated to provide the same sort of result but, whereas the rule of thumb or exposure chart cannot be misled by the nature of the subject or lighting, the exposure meter can be. When an exposure meter is used to take a reading from a small subject in a vast expanse of snow or other light-coloured background, it does not indicate 1/125 sec at *f* 16 for a 125 ASA film in bright sunlight. It is more likely to indicate 1/500 sec or less, leading to underexposure. Similarly, a predominantly dark subject may be overexposed if you follow the meter reading. This is because the meter is programmed to believe that everything it sees averages out to a mid-tone. It starts off on the wrong foot when faced with an unusual subject.

This applies equally to separate meters, built-in meters and through-the-lens meters—even the so-called spot type. The meter that reads only a small part of the scene may, in fact, be more easily misled than the meter that reads the whole screen area, because the smaller the area, the less likely that it will contain a variety of tones. The spot metering type needs to be used with extra care.

When you take a meter reading, make sure that you read an area of tones averaging out to grey. If the subject does not contain such an area change the angle of your camera or meter, provided it still measures in the same light conditions. If you cannot find a suitable area or object point the meter at the back of your hand, again positioned in such a way that the light falling on it is the same as that on the subject. The back of the hand is often a reasonable mid-tone, especially for colour photography. This is more or less equivalent to taking a reading from a standard grey card, which is a card reflecting 18% of the light falling on it.

Non-average subjects

The exposure recommendations resulting from this type of reading are suitable for virtually any subject—whatever the lighting, whatever the nature of the subject. That is not to say that it always gives perfect results. If the subject is extremely contrasty—deep shadows and strong highlights—you may lose detail in either shadows or highlights or both. With colour film you will certainly lose colour fidelity at one end or the other. Films can handle accurately only a limited range of brightnesses; subjects with a very long scale of tones receive a compromise exposure which you have to bias toward whichever end of the scale is of most importance. Generally, you tend to underexpose a little to preserve detail and colour accuracy in the highlights but there are times when shadow detail is more important. If both are equally important, you have to bring in supplementary lighting or use reflectors to brighten the shadows and so shorten the scale.

Exposure is not the problem it is so often made out to be and there is a tendency, now that meter readings are so often displayed in the viewfinder, to pay too much attention to it. If you take a careful reading when you first start shooting, there is little reason to take further readings until you have reason to believe that the light has changed. A single, straightforward reading from the subject area may not be absolutely accurate, whereas your original careful reading (preferably from a grey card or substitute) should be quite reliable. To adjust for every shot on the basis of meter needle movement is time-wasting and rather foolish.

Using the ST605 and 705 meters

The Fujica ST605 and 705 have similar metering systems but the 705 has the additional ability to measure the exposure with the lens set at its full aperture, even though the aperture ring is turned to some other setting. The 605 has to be stopped down to measure the actual amount of light that will reach the film.

The difference between the systems is that the 605 has no way of telling its meter how far the lens has been stopped down except by the intensity of the light it admits. The 705, however, has a sprung ring surrounding the lens mount and carrying a small stud. When a Fujinon lens, or other lens specifically designed for use with the Fujica ST cameras, is attached to the camera, the ring is turned to an extent dictated by the setting of the aperture ring. The lug on the back of the lens that causes the ring to turn is in a different position on lenses of different maximum aperture. So, although the aperture ring has to turn farther from, say, *f*1.8 to *f*8 than from *f*2.2 to *f*8, the teller ring round the lens mount starts from farther back for the wider aperture lens. The teller ring is thus turned to exactly the same position for *f*8 or any other aperture, no matter what the maximum aperture of the lens. Hence the positive locking position of the lens.

Metering procedure

First set the film speed. Pull up the rim of the shutter speed knob and turn it until the appropriate figure appears in the cutout. The figure (generally an ASA figure) is on the carton in which the film is packed. The figures on the scale are as follows, the italic figures being represented by dots:
25 *32 40* 50 *64 80* 100 *125 160* 200 *250 320* 400 *500 640* 800 *1000 1250* 1600 *2000 2500* 3200

Compose and focus the picture in the viewfinder and switch on the meter. On the 605, the meter switch is incorporated in the stop-down button. On the 705, light pressure on the shutter release switches on the meter.

In each case, as the meter is switched on, the needle on the right of the screen moves. For correct exposure you adjust aperture and/or shutter speed until the needle is centred in the clear area between the plus and minus signs. As you adjust the aperture on the 605, the screen darkens. On the 705 it stays at full brilliance and the needle is easier to see.

The general procedure, and the more comfortable, because your right index finger is normally on the meter switch, is to set an appropriate shutter speed first and then centre the needle by adjusting the aperture.

Varying the exposure

There may be occasions when you wish to give more or less exposure than a straight meter reading recommends. The viewfinder readout shows the extent of your over- or under-exposure directly. If the needle is at the bottom of the longer clear area, you will be one stop underexposed. If it is at the bottom of the black area, you are two stops underexposed. The top of the clear area indicates one stop overexposure and the top of the black area two stops.

Exposure meter operation

1 Set film speed. **2** Compose and focus the picture. **3** Switch on meter. **4** Check meter needle position. **5** Alter aperture to centre needle or **6** Alter shutter speed to centre needle.

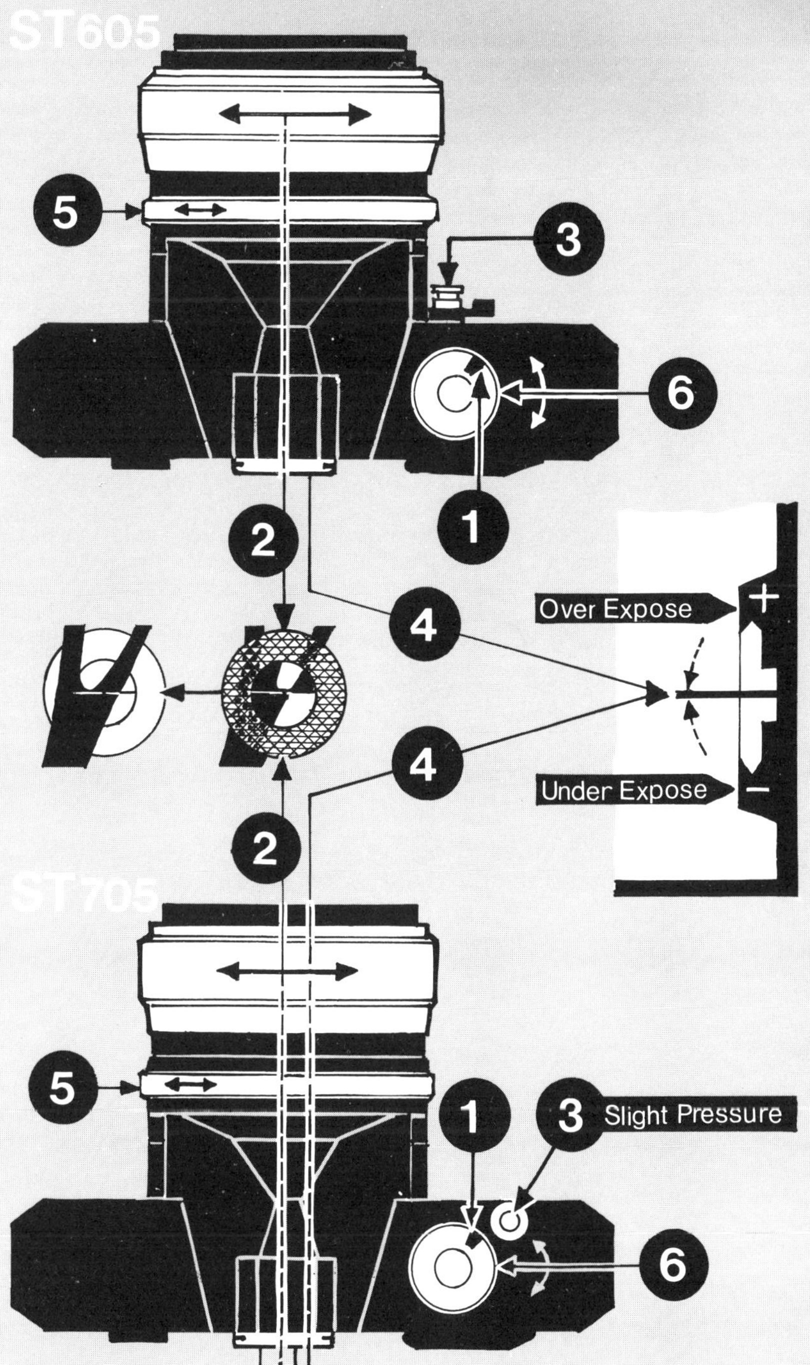
ST605
5
3
6
1
2
4
Over Expose
+
4
Under Expose
−
2
ST705
5
1
3 Slight Pressure
6

Using the ST801 meter

The metering circuit of the Fujica ST cameras is basically the same for all models. It consists of a silicon sensor on each side of the viewfinder eyepiece taking an average reading of the entire screen brightness. The resulting electrical current generated by the sensors is varied by resistances connected to shutter speed, film speed and aperture controls and amplified by a transistor circuit to provide enough power to activate the needle in the 605 and 705 or the readout LEDs in the 801 and 901.

Metering procedure

The 801 meter is a full-aperture type, like that of the 705 and operation is virtually the same.

First set the film speed by pulling up the rim of the shutter speed knob and turning it to bring the appropriate figure into the cutout. The figure (generally an ASA figure) is on the carton in which the film is packed. The figures on the scale are as follows, the italic figures being represented by dots:
25 *32 40* 50 *64 80* 100 *126 160* 200 *250 320* 400 *500 640* 800 *1000 1250* 1600 *2000 2500* 3200

Compose and focus the picture in the viewfinder and press gently on the shutter release. One or two of the LEDs on the right of the viewfinder then glows. For correct exposure, you adjust the aperture and/or shutter speed until the central, diamond-shaped LED glows. If the LED above or below it also glows, the implication is that you will obtain fractional (perhaps half a stop or less) over- or underexposure, depending on whether the second glowing LED is above or below the centre.

The general procedure, and the more comfortable because your right index finger is usually on the shutter release to keep the meter switched on, is to set a suitable shutter speed first and adjust the exposure with the lens aperture.

Varying the exposure

There may be occasions when you wish to give more or less exposure than a straight meter reading recommends. The viewfinder readout shows the extent of your over- or under-exposure directly. There are three LEDs above and below the central diamond. Each corresponds to one stop more exposure (toward the plus sign) or one stop less (toward the minus sign) than a straight meter reading recommends.

Exposure meter operation

1 Set film speed. **2** Compose and focus the picture. **3** Switch on meter. **4** Check position of glowing LED. **5** Alter aperture or **6** Alter shutter speed until central LED glows.

ST801

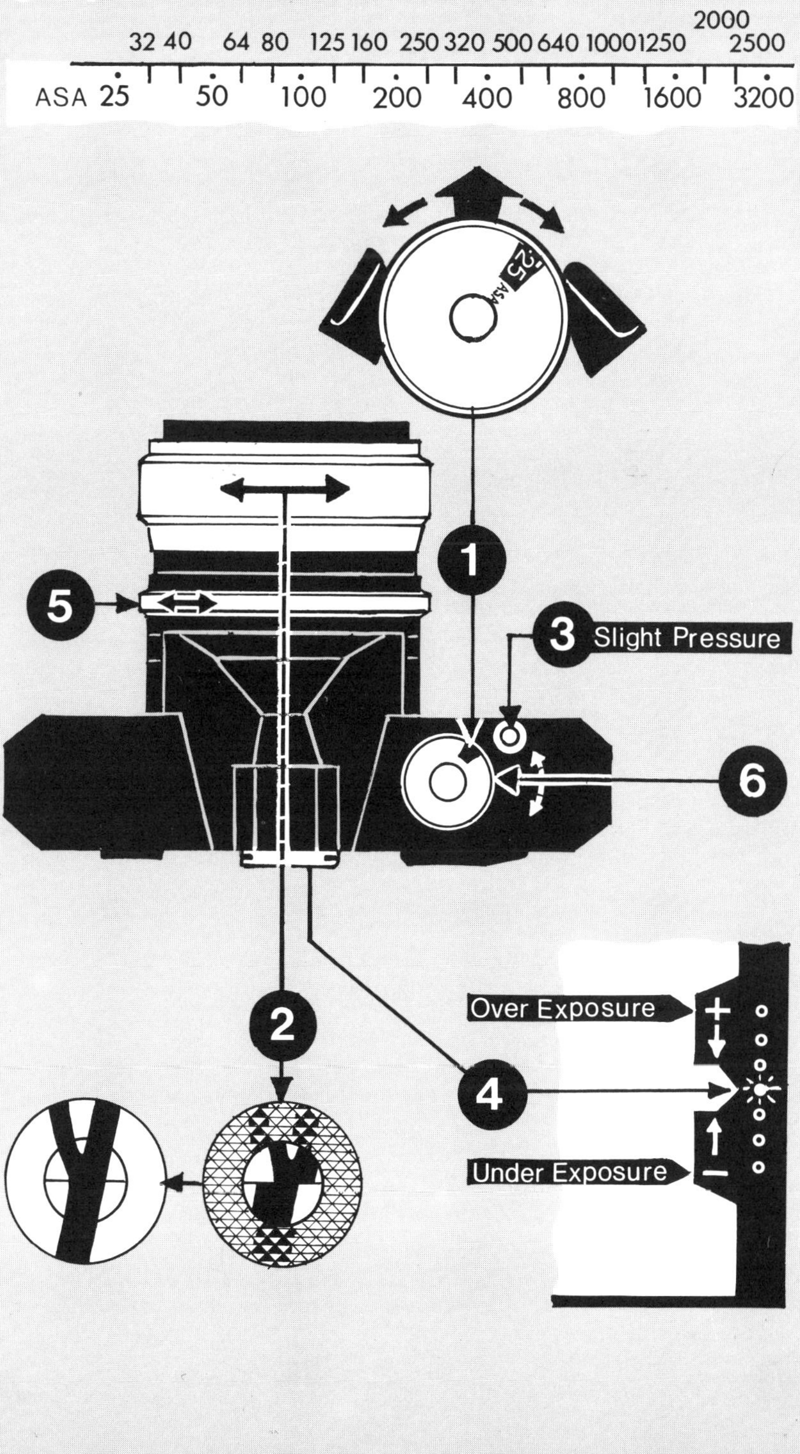

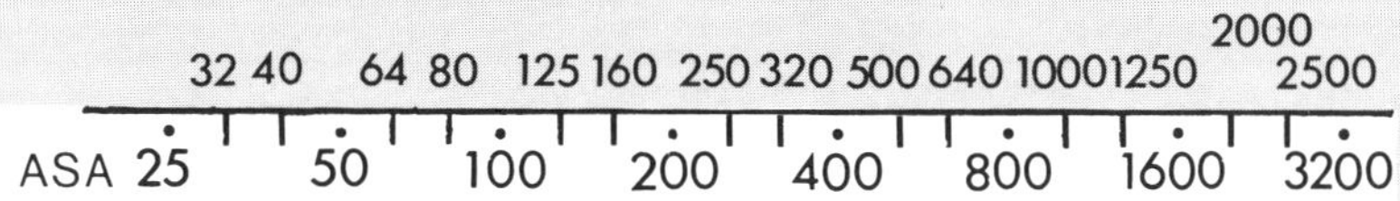

1

5

3 Slight Pressure

6

2

4

Over Exposure

Under Exposure

Using the ST901 meter

Although it uses essentially the same meter circuit as the other models, the ST901 is a more sophisticated camera. The meter is connected to an automatic shutter-speed-setting circuit instead of the connection by variable resistance to the individual shutter speed settings. Thus, as the lens aperture is varied, the meter circuit calculates the shutter speed required to suit film speed and light intensity and automatically sets the shutter to that speed – in a continuously variable range between 20 seconds and 1/1000 second. An indication of the shutter speed is shown in the form of a digital readout in the viewfinder. The range of speeds shown is:

0̄ 1000 500 200 100 60 30 10 5 2 1 2⁻5⁻10⁻20⁻

The 0̄ indicates that the light is too bright for the aperture and film speed. You must set a smaller aperture. The figures from 1000 to 1 are normal indications of shutter speed in fractions of a second. The remaining figures (with the dashes alongside) represent whole seconds. If the indication is 20 seconds and it continues to show when you open up the aperture, the light is too low for the aperture and film speed. Only if the readout can be altered by opening up the lens one stop can it be taken as a genuine 20-second reading.

The figures do not represent actual speeds. They represent a range of speeds around that shown because the shutter can give infinitely variable speeds.

Metering procedure

The meter is a full-aperture type and its operation is very simple. First set the film speed by pulling up the rim of the shutter speed knob and turning it to bring the appropriate figure into the cutout. The figure (generally an ASA figure) is on the carton in which the film is packed. The figures on the scale are as follows, the italic figures being represented by dots:

25 *32 40* 50 *64 80* 100 *125 160* 200 *250 320* 400 *500 640* 800 *1000 1250* 1600 *2000 2500* 3200

Compose and focus the picture in the viewfinder and press gently on the shutter release. Note the figure that appears above the viewfinder. If it indicates too slow a shutter speed, set a larger aperture until a more suitable speed appears. If only a slow speed can be obtained (slower than 1/60 second), it is advisable to put the camera on a tripod or use flash.

Varying the exposure

As the shutter speed setting is automatic and changes as you change the lens aperture, you cannot vary the exposure directly as on the other models. On the shutter speed dial however, on either side of the AUTO mark, there are the figures +1, +2, −1 and −2. Turning the knob to bring any of these figures opposite the index gives you one or two stops over- or under-exposure as required. To turn the knob, you have to push the small lever in front of it toward the back of the camera. The setting is then indicated on the left of the viewfinder screen.

Exposure meter operation

1 Set film speed. **2** Set shutter speed ring to AUTO. **3** Compose and focus the picture. **4** Switch on meter. **5** Check shutter speed. **6** Adjust aperture if shutter speed unsuitable (switch meter off and on for each reading). **7** When set to shutter speed index, gives two stops extra exposure. **8** One stop extra exposure. **9** One stop less exposure. **10** Two stops less exposure. The chart shows the coupling range of the ST901 meter.

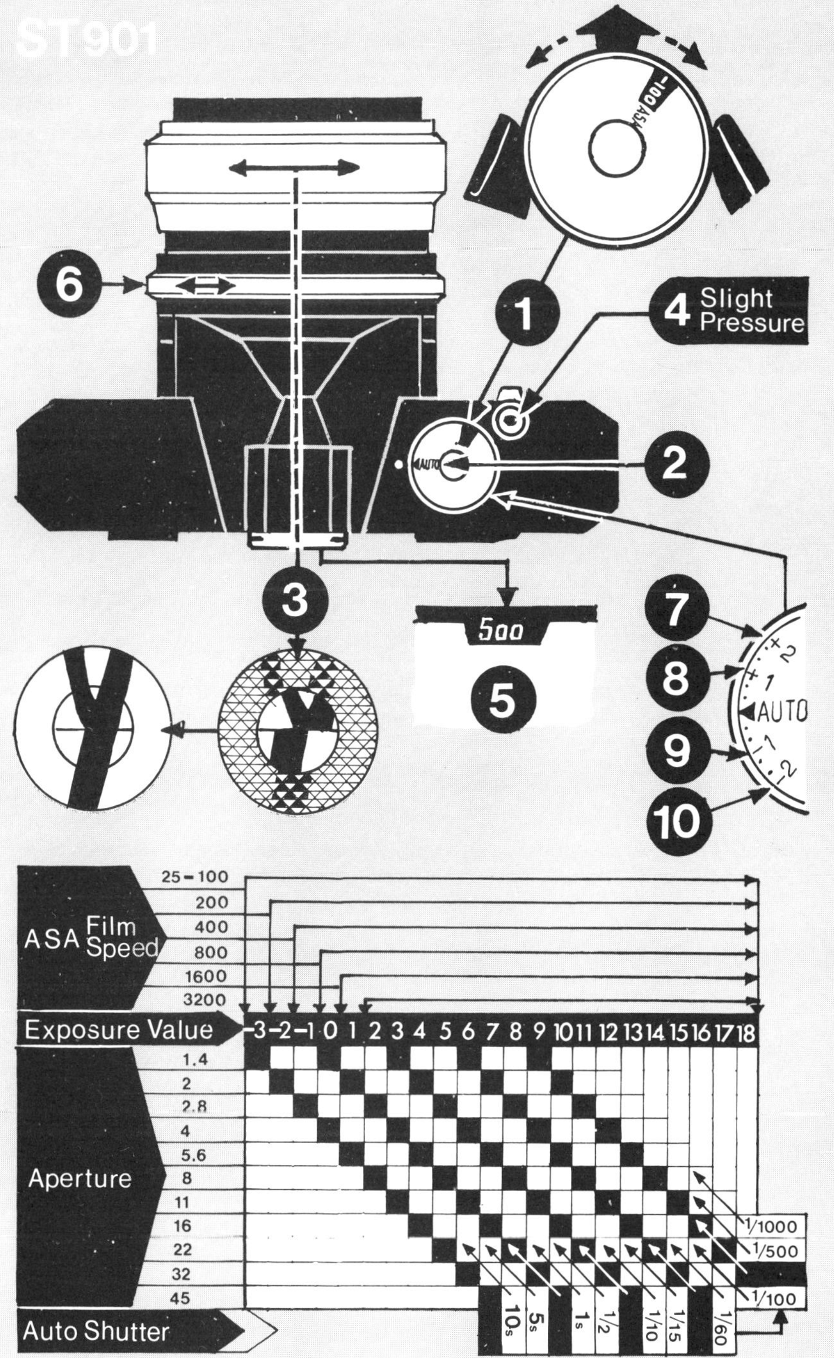
ST901
100 ASA
1
4 Slight Pressure
AUTO
2
6
3
500
5
7
8
9
10
+2
+1
AUTO
-1
-2
ASA Film Speed
25-100
200
400
800
1600
3200
Exposure Value
-3 -2 -1 0 1 2 3 4 5 6 7 8 9 10 11 12 13 14 15 16 17 18
Aperture
1.4
2
2.8
4
5.6
8
11
16
22
32
45
1/1000
1/500
1/100
Auto Shutter
10s
5s
1s
1/2
1/10
1/15
1/60

Using the AZ-1 meter

The meter circuit of the Fujica AZ-1 is a simplified version of that of the ST901. It is connected to an automatic shutter-speed-setting circuit to provide the same type of aperture-preferred automatic exposure control but the shutter speeds selected are limited to the range 1/2 second to 1/1000 second and are indicated in the viewfinder by a series of seven LEDs against a shutter speed scale. The range of speeds shown is:

1000 500 250 125 60 30 2–15 (red)

With the shutter speed knob set to AE, first pressure on the shutter release causes a LED opposite one of these figures to glow. The red 2–15 indicates that the shutter speed selected is between 1/2 and 1/15 second and the camera must therefore be rigidly supported. At this setting and at the 1000 setting, the LED may blink rapidly, indicating that the light is too low or too bright respectively for correct exposure. You must alter the aperture setting or use flash.

Metering procedure

Set the film speed by pulling up the rim of the shutter speed knob and turning it to bring the appropriate figure into the cutout. The figure (generally on the ASA scale) is on the carton in which the film is supplied. The figures on the scale are as follows, the italic figures being represented by dots:

25 *32 40* 50 *64 80* 100 *125 160* 200 *250 320* 400 *500 640* 800 *1000 1250* 1600 *2000 2500* 3200

Compose and focus the picture in the viewfinder and press gently on the shutter release. Note the position of the glowing LED. Adjust the aperture to provide a shutter speed suitable for the subject. *Lift your finger from the shutter release and then reapply first pressure for each reading.* If only a slow speed is possible (slower than 1/60 second), support the camera firmly, preferably on a tripod, or use flash.

Varying the exposure

The AZ-1 has two methods of influencing the meter's operation. When you apply first pressure to the shutter release, the meter reading is locked and, even if you change the aperture or the light changes, the shutter speed originally selected will be the one used provided you keep the shutter release half depressed up to the moment of shooting. Thus, you can take a close-up reading of a backlit subject and then move to the shooting position without affecting the exposure.

If that is not possible the +1, +2, −1, −2 settings of the shutter speed knob provide one or two stops deliberate over or under exposure as required.

Exposure meter operation

1 Set film speed. **2** Set shutter speed knob to AE. **3** Compose and focus the picture. **4** Switch on meter. **5** Check indicated shutter speed. **6** Alter aperture if shutter speed unsuitable. **7** When set to shutter speed index, gives two stops extra exposure. **8** One stop extra exposure. **9** One stop less exposure. **10** Two stops less exposure.

The chart indicates the coupling range of the AZ–1 meter.

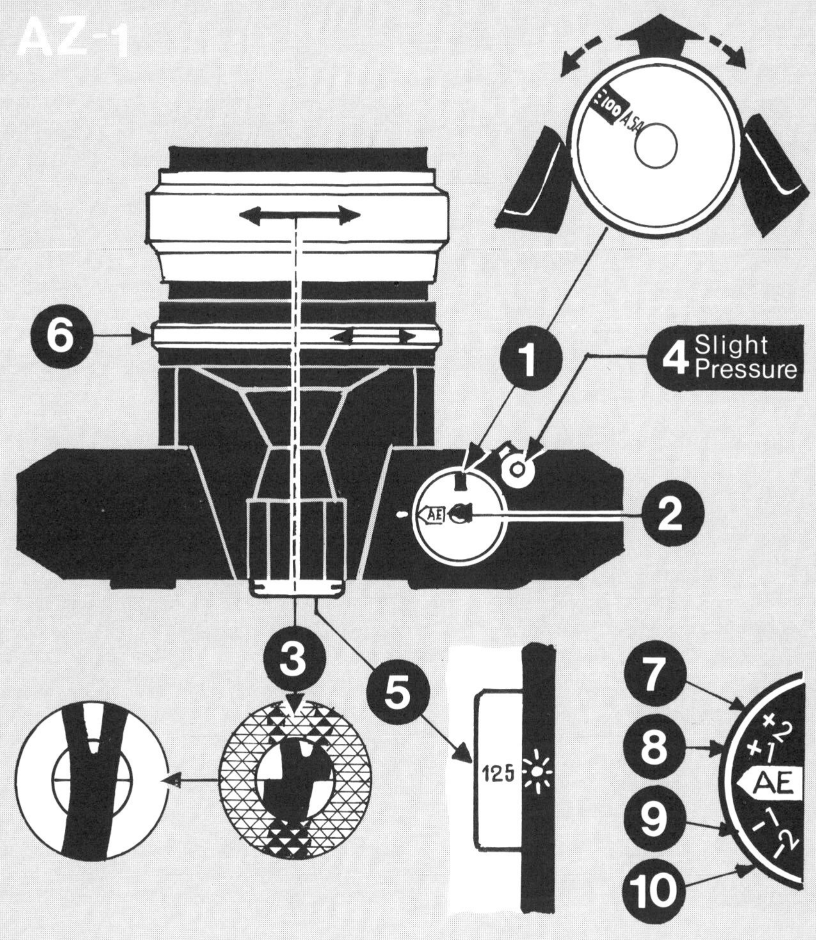

Film Speed ASA	SHUTTER SPEEDS									
	2	4	8	15	30	60	125	250	500	1000
25 - 200										
250 - 400										
500 - 800										
1000 - 1600										
2000 - 3200										

for all APERTURES from f 1.4 to f 32

Stopped-down metering

The meter of the ST605 works with the lens stopped-down to the shooting aperture. All the other models work with the lens diaphragm fully open. The aperture control moves the ring around the lens mount to indicate to the meter the extent to which the lens will be stopped down when the shutter is released.

In certain circumstances, however, even the full-aperture models have to be used with the lens stopped down, i.e. when you use lenses or behind-lens attachments (tubes, bellows, converters, etc.) that do not have the protruding lug of Fujinon lenses to move the aperture-teller ring around the lens mount. You therefore switch on the meter in the normal way but ignore the reading given at that stage. Not until you press the stop-down button on the camera front do you obtain a correct reading.

Metering procedure

The procedure is the same for all models. Set the film speed as for full aperture metering, compose and focus the picture and switch on the meter by pressing gently on the shutter release button.

Each model has its different form of readout and the ST901 and AZ-1 work automatically just as they do with full-aperture metering. First, however, before any of the models can give correct exposure you have to stop down the lens.

The stop-down button is identical in appearance on all models but operates slightly differently on the ST901. On the 705 and 801, you simply press the button directly inward. On the 901, you first have to turn it toward the lens. This is to guard against its accidental depression during automatic working.

You need two fingers on the right hand to operate both stop-down button and meter switch at the same time. As that is a rather clumsy operation, the stop-down button on the ST models (except the 605) can be locked down by turning it away from the lens while depressed. The lens diaphragm is then directly controlled by the aperture ring and opens and closes as you turn the ring. No lock is provided on the ST605 because the stop-down button is also the meter switch and leaving the meter switched on can drain the batteries rapidly. The AZ–1 button does not lock. With the meter switched on and the lens stopped down, you take your meter reading in the normal way.

Varying the exposure

The method of metering – stopped down or full aperture – should have no effect on the exposure indicated but the Fujica cameras do, in fact, seem to give a consistent half to one stop extra exposure when used in the full-aperture mode.

Varying the exposure intentionally can be carried out in exactly the same manner whether you meter at shooting or full aperture.

Stopped-down metering

1 Set film speed. **2** Attach lens and/or other accessories. **3** Depress and lock depth of field button on ST705 and 801. **4** Compose and focus the picture. **5** Set lens aperture. **6** Switch on meter. **7** On ST705 and 801, adjust shutter speed to centre meter needle or glowing LED. **8** On ST901 and AZ–1 press depth of field button to check shutter speed. Keep button depressed while you release the shutter. On the ST901, it can be locked down.

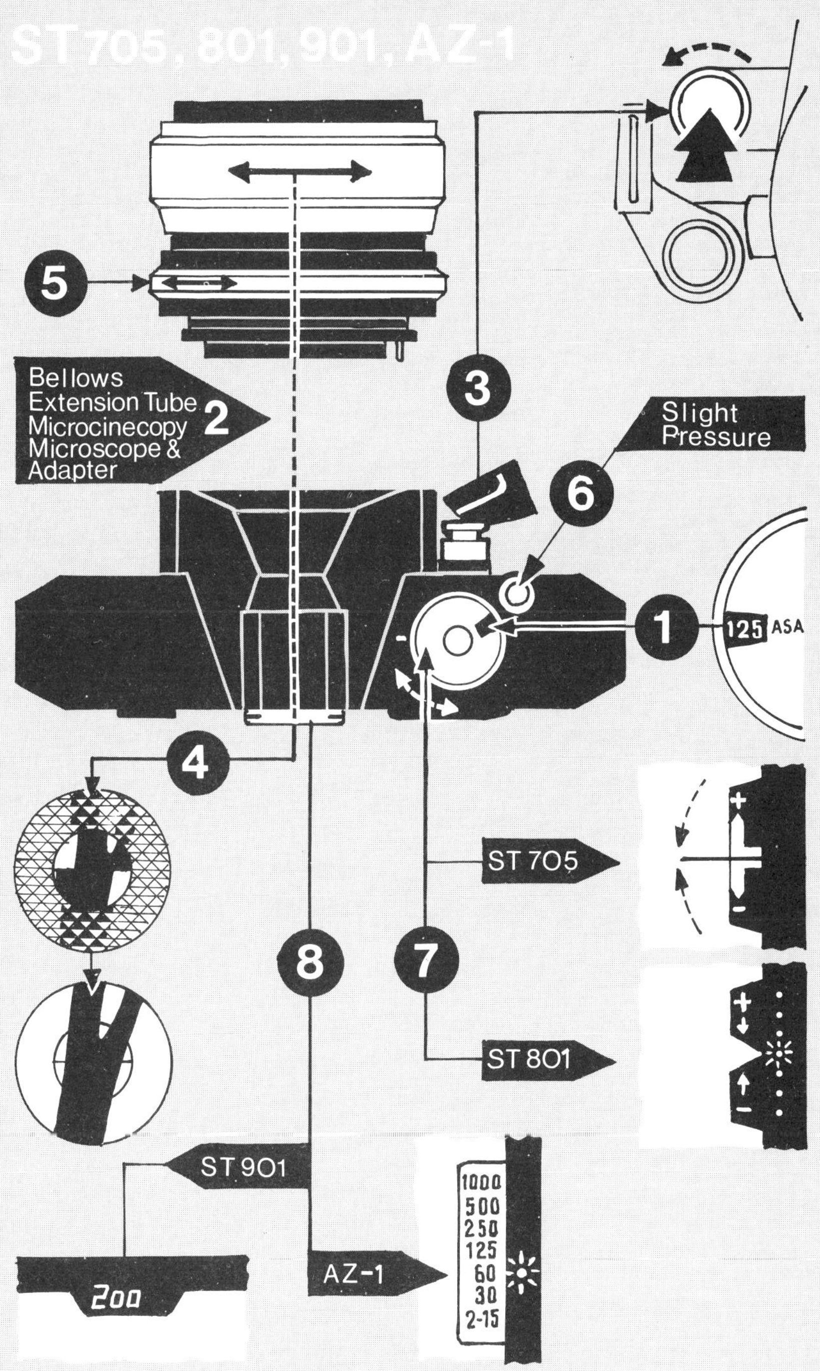
ST705, 801, 901, AZ-1
5
Bellows
Extension Tube
Microcinecopy
Microscope &
Adapter
2
3
Slight
Pressure
6
1
125 ASA
4
ST 705
+
-
8
7
ST 801
ST 901
AZ-1
200
1000
500
250
125
60
30
2-15

Holding the camera

One of the most common causes of unsharp pictures is camera shake, i.e. movement of the camera during exposure. While the picture is being taken, an image of the subject is projected by the lens on to the film. If the camera moves, even imperceptibly, while the shutter is open, the image is displaced on the film and forms a double or multiple image. In most cases, the movement is so fractional that the different images are indistinguishable. The result is, however, a thickening of fine lines and an enlargement of small detail, producing an image less sharp than the camera is capable of producing.

Thus, every precaution must be taken at all times to hold the camera completely still – even when using the fastest shutter speeds. At slower speeds the risk of movement is naturally greater but blur induced by camera shake is possible even at 1/1000 sec.

Generally, the steadiest hold is provided when the photographer stands straight, with the legs slightly apart and the weight distributed equally on each leg. The camera should be held firmly but not too tightly in both hands with the arms against the sides and elbows well in.

Horizontal and vertical holds

The easiest grip for horizontal pictures is as shown opposite. The left hand operates focusing, shutter speed and aperture controls as well as the meter switch. The right hand winds on the film and releases the shutter.

The grip for vertical pictures can be as shown, with the first or second finger of the right hand releasing the shutter, or the hands can be reversed with the camera the other way up and the thumb on the release button.

Always take advantage of any support that may be available by resting the camera or the elbows on a wall, chairback, etc. or by leaning against a tree, lamp-post or other support, or even by lying prone and propping the elbows on the ground. Sometimes you may be able to place the camera on a convenient support and let the self-timer release the shutter.

Remember that it needs only a fractional displacement of the image to produce unsharp pictures. Therefore, the narrower angle of view of longer focal length lenses can induce blur with considerably less camera movement than if a shorter focus lens were used.

The camera must be absolutely steady for sharp pictures

Camera shake is the enemy of truly sharp pictures. Cultivate an easy stance and steady hold so that the camera can be held perfectly still at the moment of exposure.

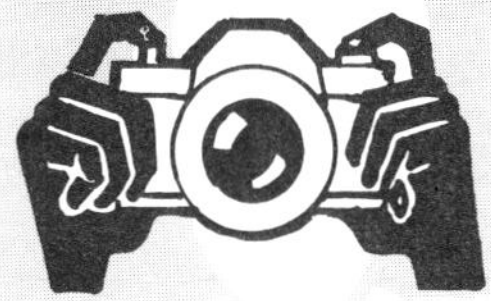

Tuck IN

Tuck IN

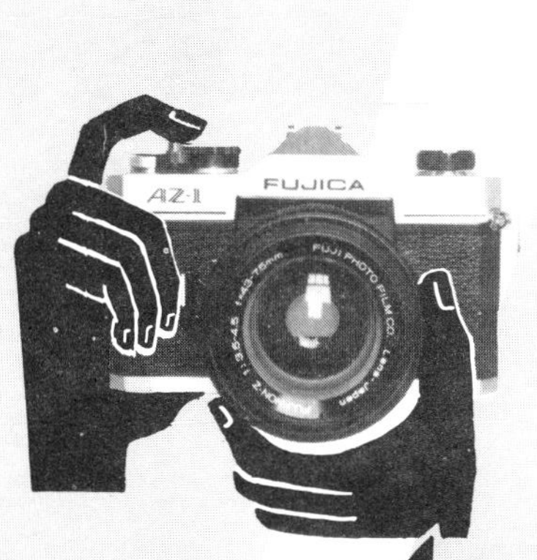

Firmly Placed

Camera supports

When it is convenient to do so, it is always advisable to mount the camera on a tripod or other firm support. Most people overestimate their ability to hold a camera still at the moment of exposure and many never realise that their pictures could be a great deal sharper than they are.

There are many models of tripod and not a few of them are far too flimsy to be of any use with a comparatively lightweight 35 mm camera. Your tripod should be of stout construction with solidly locking legs that have no tendency to bend or whip under firm pressure on the top. If a centre column is fitted it must ride smoothly without too much play and be impossible to force down when locked. The camera platform should preferably be a large pan-and-tilt rather than a ball and socket.

Miniature tripod

The smaller stand is useful in many situations where a full size tripod cannot be accommodated. It can rest on a table, chair, wall, car roof, etc. and provide adequate support for long exposures. Similar small supports with clamps, spikes and other methods of securing them are supplied by various manufacturers and can be of great value where longer exposures are necessary.

Another type of support that sometimes helps to hold long lenses steady is the pistol grip, although its greatest value is probably in conjunction with a support for the left hand so that the barrel of the lens can be laid across the left elbow. The pistol grip usually has a built in cable release to allow the shutter to be fired from its trigger.

Cable release

This is a plunger type release which screws into the shutter button for tripod mounted shots, because finger pressure on the shutter release could quite easily set up vibrations in the tripod. For long time exposures with the shutter speed dial at B a cable release with a lock-down facility is valuable. You need not then hold onto the release throughout the exposure.

The mounting on top of the tripod takes many forms, too, but the most popular are the ball and socket, allowing the camera to be tilted in almost any direction, and the pan-and-tilt, which allows only an up-and-down tilt or a 360-degree horizontal swivel. The pan-and-tilt usually has a larger mounting platform for the camera and more positive locking.

Camera supports

A Clamp and mini-tripod. **B** Pistol grip with cable release. **C** Ball and socket head. **D** Table tripod.

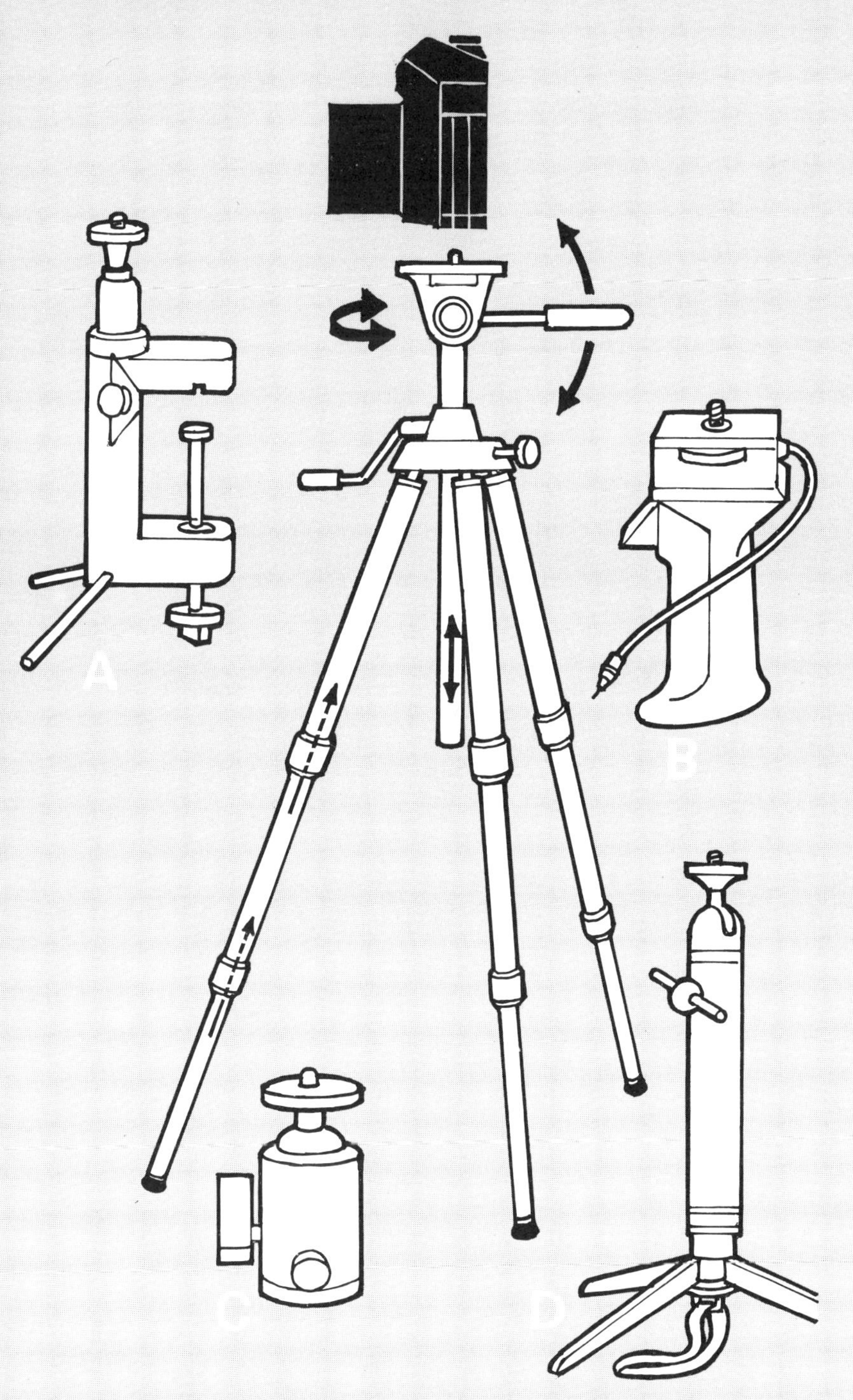
A
B
C
D

Loading the Fujica SLRs

To load a film into your Fujica camera, you must first open the camera back. Unlock the back cover by pulling the rewind knob firmly upward against spring pressure at the end of its travel. The back then pops partially open and you can fold it back completely to the right. Pull up the rewind knob so that the prong clears the film chamber. Take a loaded film cassette and place it in the film chamber below the rewind knob with the protruding knob of the central spool at the bottom. Push the rewind knob fully back, twisting it to and fro if necessary to engage the spindle of the cassette spool.

Draw the film leader out of the cassette and take it across the back of the camera until you can push the tip of the film leader into one of the slots in the take-up spool. Push it in as far as possible. Operate the film transport lever once, holding the cassette down with your thumb. Make sure that the film is still attached to the take-up spool and that the sprockets on the spindle next to it are engaging the perforations in the film.

Close the camera back and press it until it clicks into the locked position. Release the shutter and transport the film twice to wind off the film fogged while you had the back open. Check that the rewind knob rotates during this operation, indicating that the film is being pulled out of the cassette.

It is advisable to set the ST901 shutter to a manual speed for this operation. If you leave it on automatic in low light or with the lens cap on, the meter automatically sets a long, perhaps 20-second, exposure.

Finally, set the film speed. Pull up the rim of the shutter speed knob and turn it until the required figure shows in the cutout. The figure to set (ASA or DIN, according to the marking on the shutter speed knob) is shown on the carton in which the film is packed.

Loading the camera

1 Open camera back. **2** Insert film cassette. **3** Push back rewind knob. **4** Insert film leader into take-up spool slot. **5** Operate transport lever once. **6** Check that sprockets are engaging film perforations. **7** Close camera back. **8** Set ST901 and AZ–1 to manual shutter speed. **9** Operate transport lever and release shutter alternately to bring No 1 (white dot) opposite the frame counter index. **10** Set film speed. **11** The ST901 shows the film type (for Fuji films) in the window in the camera back.

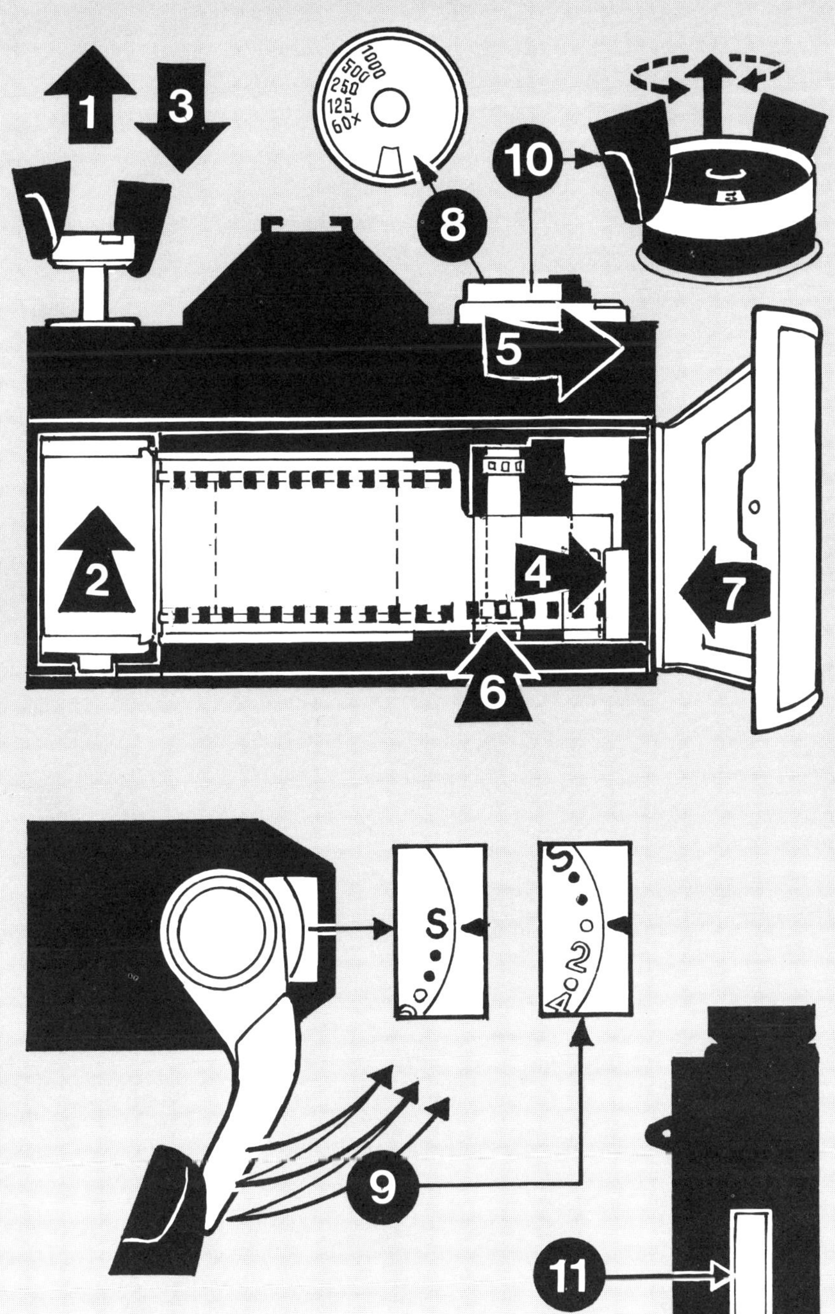

1
3
1000
500
250
125
60x
8
10
5
2
4
7
6
S
2
4
9
11

Black-and-white films

The vast majority of black-and-white films are processed to produce negatives. They consist of an emulsion of silver halides in gelatin, coated on a transparent flexible base. When this is exposed correctly, it forms an invisible *latent* image. During development the visible image of silver particles forms. The silver is deposited in proportion to the light which was focused on the film from the subject. Thus the negative is dark where the subject was light, and vice versa. When a print is made from a negative, silver is deposited in the print emulsion in proportion to the light passing through the negative and thus depicts the tones of the original subject. The characteristics of a negative depend on the type of film used, and on the processing it is given.

Grain

When a negative is magnified, it is possible to see the clumps of silver grains that form the image. This is called the grain or graininess of the negative and is proportional to the film speed; that is, the faster a film, the greater will be its grain. The grain is also influenced by the exposure and processing used. Any deviation from the normal recommendations for the film and developer—especially over-exposing or over-developing—is likely to lead to increased grain.

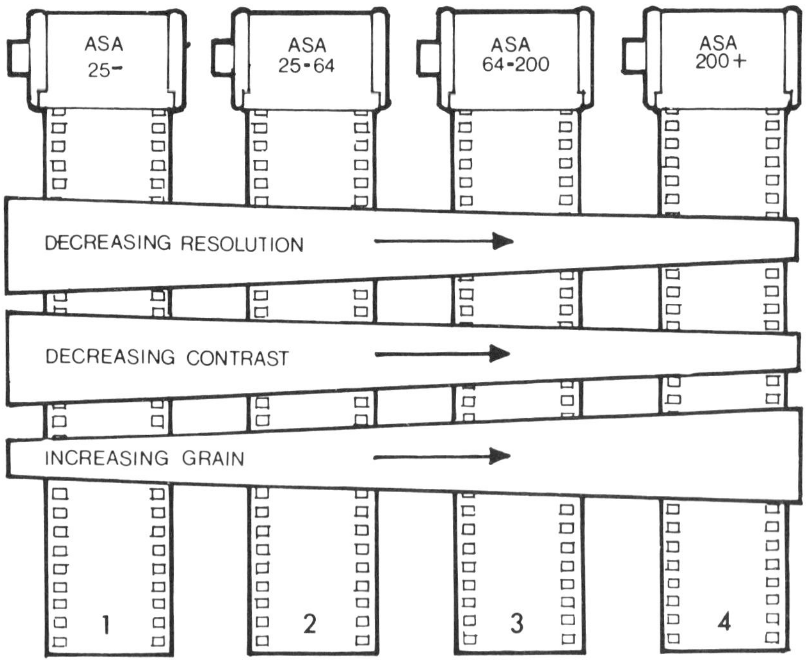

Generally speaking, films of low sensitivity to light are formed from smaller and more evenly spaced silver halide grains. Thus, the slower the film, the less noticeable the granular structure on enlargement and the higher the resolution. Common uses are: 1, very slow films, fine copying work. 2, slow films, static or brilliantly lit subjects. 3, medium speed, average photography. 4, fast, low-light photography.

Contrast

The range of grey tones a film can produce between black and white is called its contrast. Extremely high contrast materials record most of a subject as either black or white, whereas low contrast materials can give a wide range of greys between the two extremes. Normal camera films all have an acceptable contrast for general pictorial use, although the more contrasty ones give less highlight and shadow detail in pictures of high contrast subjects. As a rule, the faster a film, the lower its contrast. Prolonging the processing increases the contrast at the expense of increasing the grain.

Colour sensitivity

Untreated silver halides are sensitive only to blue light (and ultraviolet radiation). Modern photographic emulsions incorporate dyes which make them sensitive to other colours. General-purpose camera films have a sensitivity roughly the same as the human eye—and are designated *panchromatic*. High speed films have an extended red sensitivity, and some specialised emulsions are sensitive either only to blue, or to blue and green. The latter are called *orthochromatic*. The reaction of a film to different colours can be altered by the use of filters.

Exposure latitude

The best negatives are produced when the film is given the optimum exposure. However, errors of up to one stop make little difference, and printable negatives can be produced with exposures up to three stops away from the ideal, but such negatives are more difficult to print. They also have little shadow detail, if they are underexposed, or little highlight detail if they are overexposed— nor do they give as good enlargements as correctly exposed negatives. Deviation from normal processing recommendations may alter the effective speed, and special processing may be used to "retrieve" drastically mis-exposed films. It does not, however, give excellent results.

Other characteristics

Film manufacturers refer to the *acutance* or edge sharpness and *resolving power* of their films. These are two characteristics which affect the sharpness of a photographic image, but all modern films produce so sharp an image that they are characteristics of interest only in specialist applications. All modern general-purpose films also carry an anti-halation backing to prevent light that has passed through the emulsion being reflected back and degrading the image.

Choice of film

The contrast and graininess of a negative determine the degree to which the image can be enlarged. For most purposes a medium speed film (80–160 ASA, 20–23 DIN) will prove ideal. Carefully processed 35 mm negatives can yield virtually grain-free prints up to 15 × 12 inches. Slow films (20–40 ASA, 11–14 DIN) are best if you need big enlargements, and fast films 400–500 ASA, 27–28 DIN) are needed for dull conditions or fast action photography. Films faster than this (or special processing for extra speed) usually give unacceptably grainy images, and should be avoided except when there is no alternative.

Colour films

There are two types of colour film in common use—negative and reversal. Negative films are processed to produce images which are reversed in both colour and tone from the original subject. These are then used to produce colour prints. Reversal films are processed to produce a positive image closely resembling the original subject. The image is viewed either by transmitted light or projected on to a screen.

How they work

When a colour film is exposed, it produces a latent image in the same way as a black-and-white film. During processing, this is converted to a coloured dye image, the dyes being formed together with silver grains. The silver is then removed to leave the coloured dyes. In a colour negative film, the dyes correspond to the silver formed from the original latent image. They are designed also to be of complementary (opposite) colours to the original subject. In a reversal film, the original latent image is developed, and the film then re-exposed to light. On re-development, coloured dyes are produced only when (and where) the second image develops.

Exposure latitude

Just like black-and-white films, colour films must be given the right exposure. This is particularly important for reversal films, because there is no intermediate printing stage. The density of the final transparency is determined by the exposure in the

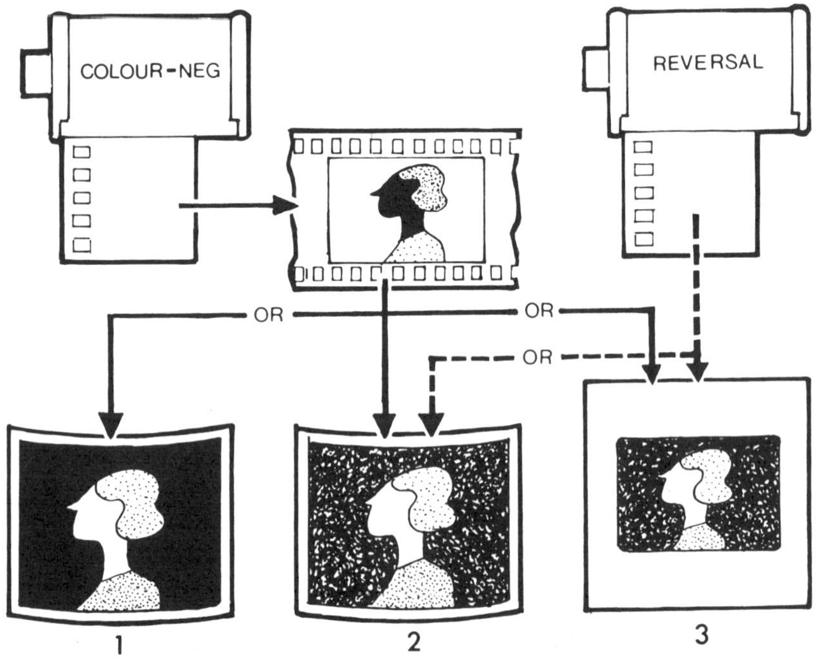

Colour negative film is for colour prints (2) *but colour slides* (3) *or black-and-white prints* (1) *can be made. Colour reversal film is for slides but can be used for prints, too.*

camera, which for optimum results should be correct to within half a stop. Colour negative films can produce adequate colour representation if over exposed up to two stops, or underexposed one stop. Film manufacturers supply meter settings (ASA and DIN ratings) for colour films. These will give normal results but, like any other exposure recommendation, should be modified to suit your equipment and viewing preferences.

Colour of lighting

Lighting varies greatly in colour, from the almost red light of an open fire to the strong blue of a blue sky (without sunlight). Normal daylight is a mixture of blue skylight and yellow sunlight. Our eyes adapt to the colour of lighting, but colour films do not. Compensation can be made when printing from colour negatives, but transparency films must be balanced for the light source in use. Manufacturers produce different types: Daylight—for use in daylight and with electronic flash or blue flashbulbs; Tungsten, Type A—for photolamps (3400 K) and Type B for use with studio lamps or tungsten halogen lamps (3200 K). A white object lit by a 60 watt bulb and and pictured on a daylight type film comes out a bright orange colour; whereas lit by daylight it comes out blue on a tungsten light film. Filters are available to provide correct colour balance when using a film in lighting other than that for which it is balanced.

Film speeds and image qualities

As their speed rises, colour films increase in graininess, while decreasing in contrast and colour saturation. The change in graininess and contrast being more marked than it is on black-and-white films for the same change in film speeds. Because the grain is multi-coloured, it may be considered more objectionable than that on black-and-white photographs. All commonly available colour negative films are of moderate speed (64–100 ASA, 19–21 DIN), and give results comparable with medium speed black-and-white films. Transparency films are available in slow (20–32 ASA, 14–16 DIN), moderate (64–100 ASA, 19–21 DIN) and fast (160–200 ASA, 23–24 DIN). Faster films and special processing should be reserved for cases of necessity. Many photographers use the slowest possible transparency films to give them the greatest colour saturation and sharpest images. This is particularly important if any of the pictures are to be offered for reproduction. The fast films have a distinguishable grain, but this is not noticeable at normal projection distances.

Choice of film type

Apart from the choice of (reversal) film speed, one must choose between reversal and negative films for any particular use.

Colour transparencies are ideal for group viewing, and projected images are more closely comparable to the original than are prints. They are also suitable for use as originals for photomechanical reproduction. The finest colour prints can be made from transparencies, but they are extremely expensive. Conventional colour prints made from transparencies, however, are not usually as good as those made from colour negatives.

Colour negatives can be printed directly to give either prints or transparencies of equal quality. Negative films are thus the first choice for making prints or when the final form is undecided. The main disadvantage of negative films is the cost of printing. This can be significantly reduced, however, by making (or having made) only those prints you want to keep. A number of laboratories will process a film and return it with a contact sheet so that you can select the negatives before any prints are made.

Shooting with the Fujica ST605 and 705

Having loaded the camera and set the film speed, you are ready to take pictures. Although the ST605 is a stopped-down metering type and the 705 works at full aperture, the procedure is basically the same.

First, unlock the shutter release of the 705 by pulling it upward and turning it anti-clockwise. The shutter release should always be locked when you put the camera away because it is also the meter switch. The 605 has no shutter release lock because its meter switch is incorporated in the stop-down button.

Remove the lens cap and, looking through the viewfinder eyepiece, compose your picture carefully on the screen and focus sharply. Switch on the meter by taking up the first pressure on the shutter release of the 705 or by pressing the stop-down button of the 605. The needle on the right of the viewfinder should move. For correct exposure, you must adjust the shutter speed and/or aperture to bring the needle to the centre of the clear area.

It is generally most convenient to set a shutter speed to suit the subject first and then centre the needle by altering the aperture with your left hand.

When the needle is centred, aperture and shutter speed are set for correct exposure of a subject with normal tone distribution in most lighting conditions. Press the shutter release gently and take the picture.

As the ST605 is a stopped-down metering camera, the screen image darkens as you switch on the exposure meter – unless the lens is set to full aperture. If lighting conditions are such that you can then see the needle only with difficulty, meter at full aperture and then calculate the exposure required at a smaller aperture and set the camera controls accordingly.

The ST705 meters at full aperture in normal practice but can also be used as a stopped-down type when necessary (see page 56).

After you have taken the picture, wind on the film ready for the next shot and, unless you are continuing to shoot, replace the lens cap. When you finish shooting, lock the shutter release of the ST705 by pulling it upward and turning it clockwise.

Shooting procedure

1 Unlock shutter release (ST705). **2** Remove lens cap. **3** Compose and focus the picture. **4, 4A** Switch on meter. **5** Check meter needle position and centre by adjusting aperture. **6** or shutter speed. **7, 8** Release shutter. **9** Transport film.

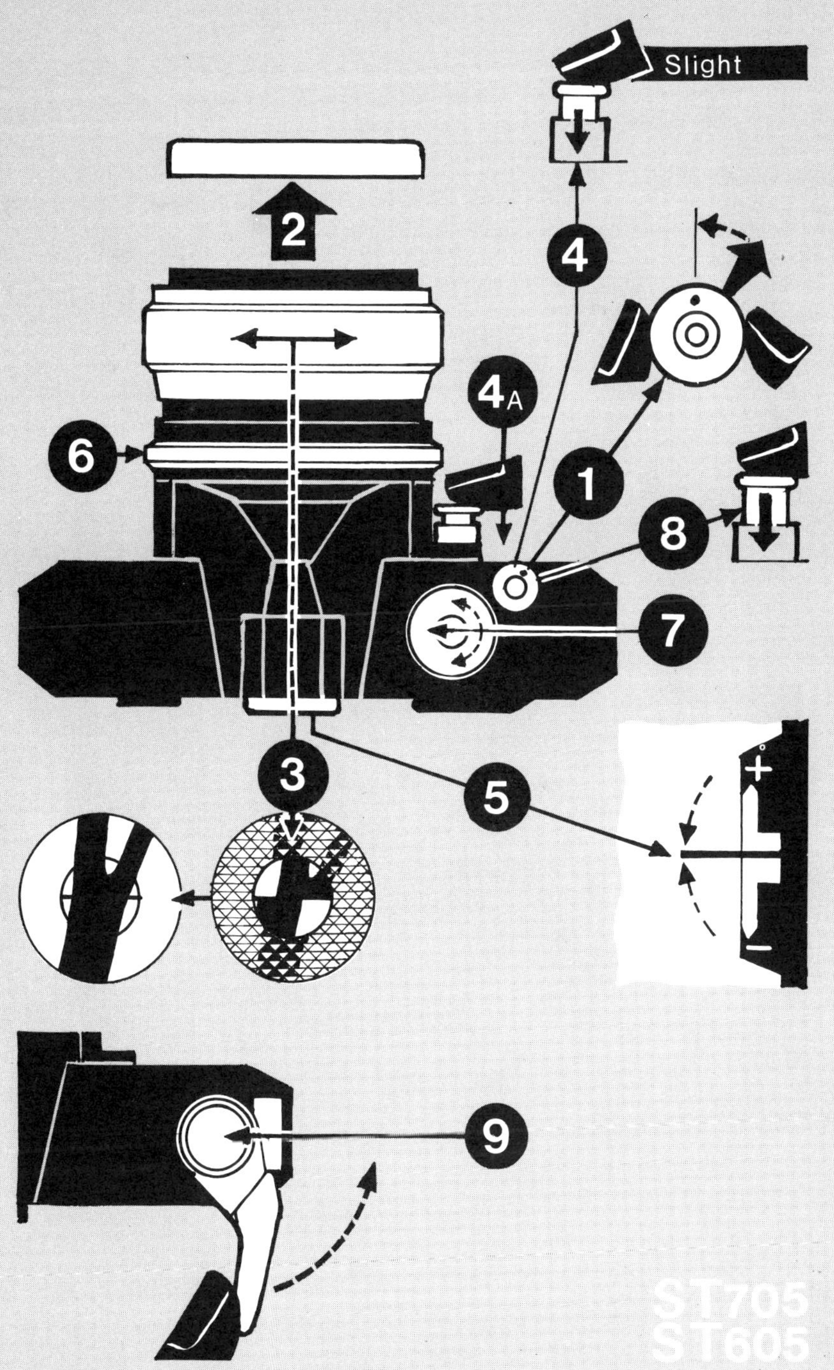

ST705
ST605

Shooting with the Fujica ST801

Having loaded the camera and set the film speed you are ready to take pictures. First unlock the shutter release knob by pulling it upward and turning it anti-clockwise. The shutter release should always be locked when you put the camera away because it is also the meter switch.

Remove the lens cap and, looking through the viewfinder eyepiece, compose the picture carefully on the screen and focus sharply. Switch the meter on by taking up the first pressure on the shutter release. One of the LEDs on the right of the view-finder should then glow. For correct exposure, you must adjust shutter speed and/or aperture until the central, diamond-shaped LED glows. The shutter speed you set is indicated on the left of the viewfinder screen.

It is generally most convenient to set a shutter speed to suit the subject first and then adjust the aperture until the central LED glows. Occasionally, the LED above or below the centre also glows but, provided the central LED is the brighter, your exposure will be sufficiently accurate.

When the central LED is glowing, aperture and shutter speed are set for correct exposure of a subject with normal tone distribution in most lighting conditions. Press the shutter release and take the picture.

The Fujica ST801 normally meters at full aperture. In certain circumstances, however, you have to use the meter in the stopped-down mode. The procedure is detailed on page 56. As a general practice, you should not use a lens designed for full-aperture metering in the stopped-down mode. It is liable to be a little optimistic about the exposure required.

After you have taken the picture, wind on the film ready for the next shot and, unless you are continuing to shoot, replace the lens cap. When you finish shooting, lock the shutter release by pulling it upward and turning it clockwise.

Shooting procedure

1 Unlock shutter release. **2** Remove lens cap. **3** Compose and focus the picture. **4** Switch on meter. **5** Adjust aperture, or **6** Adjust shutter speed until **7** Correct exposure is indicated in the viewfinder. **8** Release shutter. **9** Transport film.

ST 801

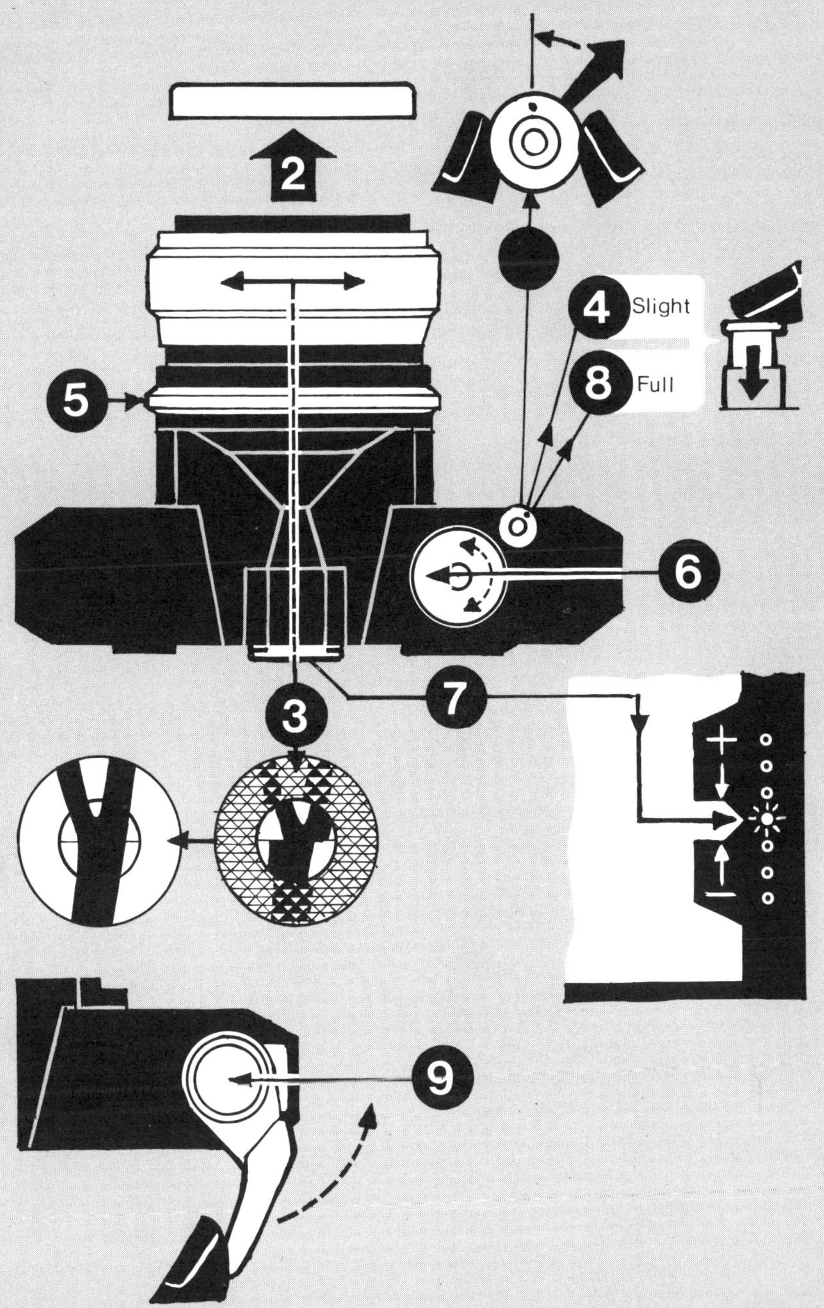

Shooting with the Fujica ST901

Having loaded the camera and set the film speed you are ready to take pictures. First unlock the shutter release knob by turning the switch surrounding it so that the green dot points forward. The shutter release should always be locked when you put the camera away because it is also the meter switch.

Remove the lens cap and, looking through the viewfinder eyepiece, compose the picture carefully on the screen and focus sharply. Switch the meter on by taking up the first pressure on the shutter release. The digital readout above the viewfinder screen should then glow and indicate the approximate shutter speed that the meter will set automatically as soon as you fully depress the shutter release. If it does not, the battery is exhausted or wrongly loaded, or the shutter speed knob is on a manual setting. The speed set is then indicated on the left of the viewfinder screen.

You could shoot immediately, of course, provided the readout was not 20⁻ or 0⁻, but you should check that the shutter speed is suitable for the subject and for hand-held shooting. If it is 1/30 second or slower, you must take every precaution to keep the camera absolutely still during the exposure. That normally means putting it on a tripod or other solid support.

In practice, it is generally convenient for most subjects to vary the aperture until the readout indicates a shutter speed of 1/1000 second or faster. Alternatively, in normal daylight shooting, you can set an aperture of *f*5.6 or *f*8 or *f*11, depending on film speed and the general light level, and be reasonably certain that the meter will set a sufficiently fast shutter speed for hand-held shooting. You need then only check the readout occasionally if the light appears to be changing. Once you are satisfied that the indicated shutter speed is suitable for the subject, press the shutter release gently and take the picture.

The Fujica ST901 normally meters at full aperture but can be used in the stopped-down mode when necessary (see page 56). As a general practice, however, it is advisable not to use lenses designed for full-aperture metering in the stopped-down mode. They tend to be a little optimistic about the exposure required.

When you have taken your picture, wind the film on for the next exposure and, unless you are continuing to shoot, replace the lens cap. When you finish shooting, lock the shutter release.

Using manually-set-shutter speeds

Exceptionally, the ST901 can be used with manual setting of shutter speeds between 1/60 and 1/1000 second or on the B setting. You can set these speeds by pressing the lock lever in front of the shutter speed knob inward (toward the back of the camera) while turning the shutter speed knob to release it from the AUTO position. The shutter speed set then appears on the left of the viewfinder and the digital readout does not operate because the battery is connected only in the AUTO position and neither the exposure meter nor the electronic control of shutter speeds can work without battery power.

Shooting procedure

1 Unlock shutter release. **2** Remove lens cap. **3** Set shutter speed knob to AUTO. **4** Compose and focus the picture. **5** Switch on meter. **6** Adjust aperture until required shutter speed **7** is indicated in the viewfinder. **8** Release shutter. **9** Transport film.

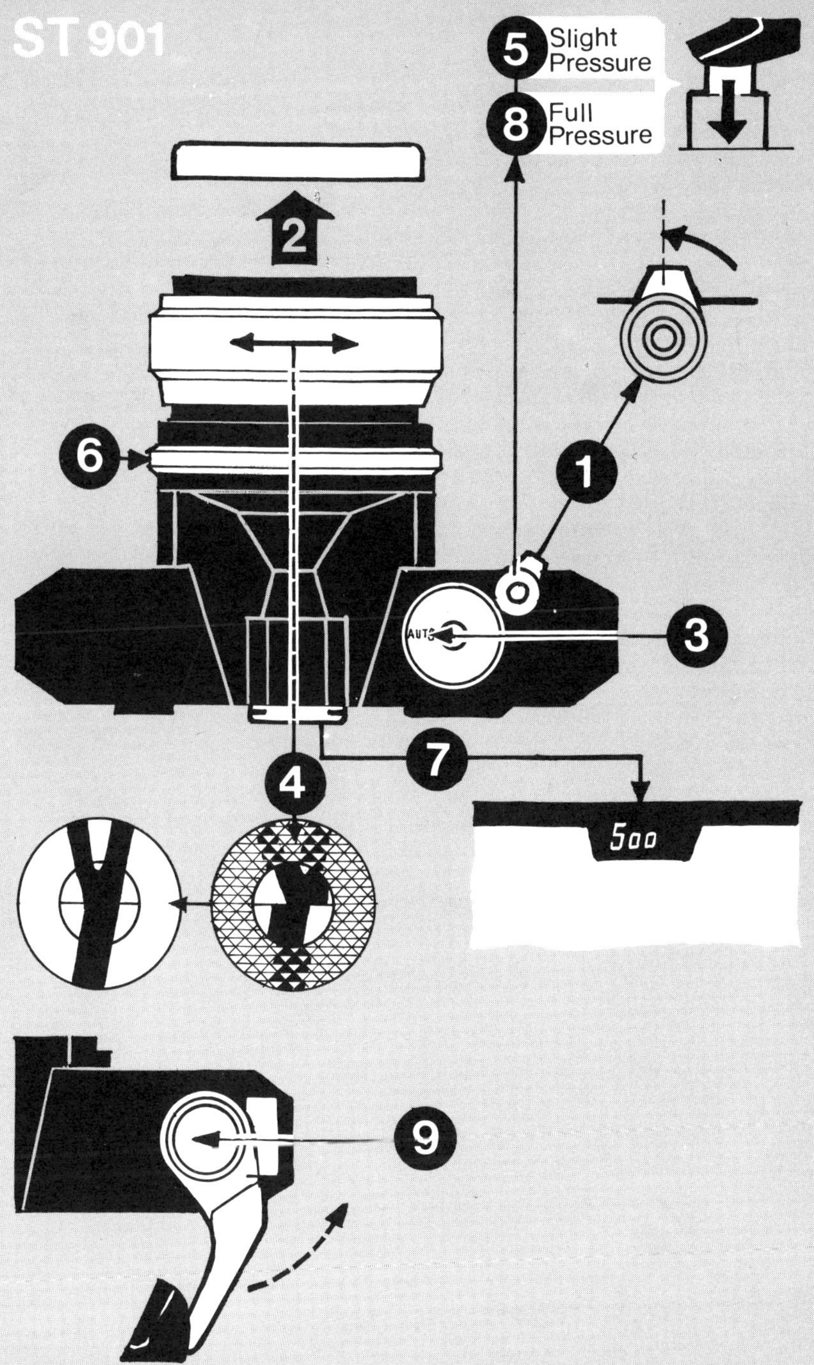

ST 901
5 Slight Pressure
8 Full Pressure
2
6
1
AUTO
3
7
4
500
9

Shooting with Fujica AZ-1

Having loaded the camera and set the film speed you are ready to take pictures. First unlock the shutter speed knob by turning the switch surrounding it away from the L position. The shutter release should always be locked when you put the camera away because it is also the meter switch.

Remove the lens caps and, looking through the viewfinder eyepiece, compose the picture carefully and focus sharply. Switch on the meter by taking up the first pressure on the shutter release. One of the seven LEDs on the right of the screen should then glow to indicate the shutter speed selected. If no LED glows, the batteries are exhausted or wrongly loaded, or the shutter speed knob is on a manual setting.

Check the shutter speed and aperture settings to make sure that they suit the subject. If the shutter speed indicated is 1/30 second or slower, support the camera as rigidly as possible during the exposure or use flash. If the top or bottom LED blinks rapidly change the aperture until you get a steady light. *Let go of the shutter release button and reapply first pressure for each reading.*

In most circumstances, you can adjust the aperture to indicate a shutter speed of 1/125 second or faster; or, in good daylight, an aperture setting of *f*5.6, *f*8 or *f*11, depending on the film speed, will ensure a suitable shutter speed for hand-held shots. You need check the readout only occasionally when the light appears to be changing.

When you are satisfied with aperture and shutter speed settings, press the shutter release fully downward to take the picture.

The Fujica AZ-1 normally meters at full aperture, but it can be used in the stopped-down mode when necessary (see page 56). It is not advisable to use lenses designed for full-aperture metering in the stopped-down mode. They tend to give optimistic readings.

When you have taken your picture, wind on the film for next exposure and, unless you are continuing to shoot, replace the lens cap. When you finish shooting, lock the shutter release by turning the switch around the button to the L position.

Using manually-set shutter speeds

If your batteries are exhausted, you can use the AZ-1 manually by turning the shutter speed knob to 60, 250 or 1000. The 60 position is commonly used with flash. When you use the camera manually, the meter circuit is disconnected.

Shooting procedure

1 Unlock shutter release. **2** Remove lens cap. **3** Set shutter speed knob to AE. **4** Compose and focus the picture. **5** Set aperture required. **6** Switch on meter. **7** Check shutter speed. **8** Release shutter. **9** Transport film.

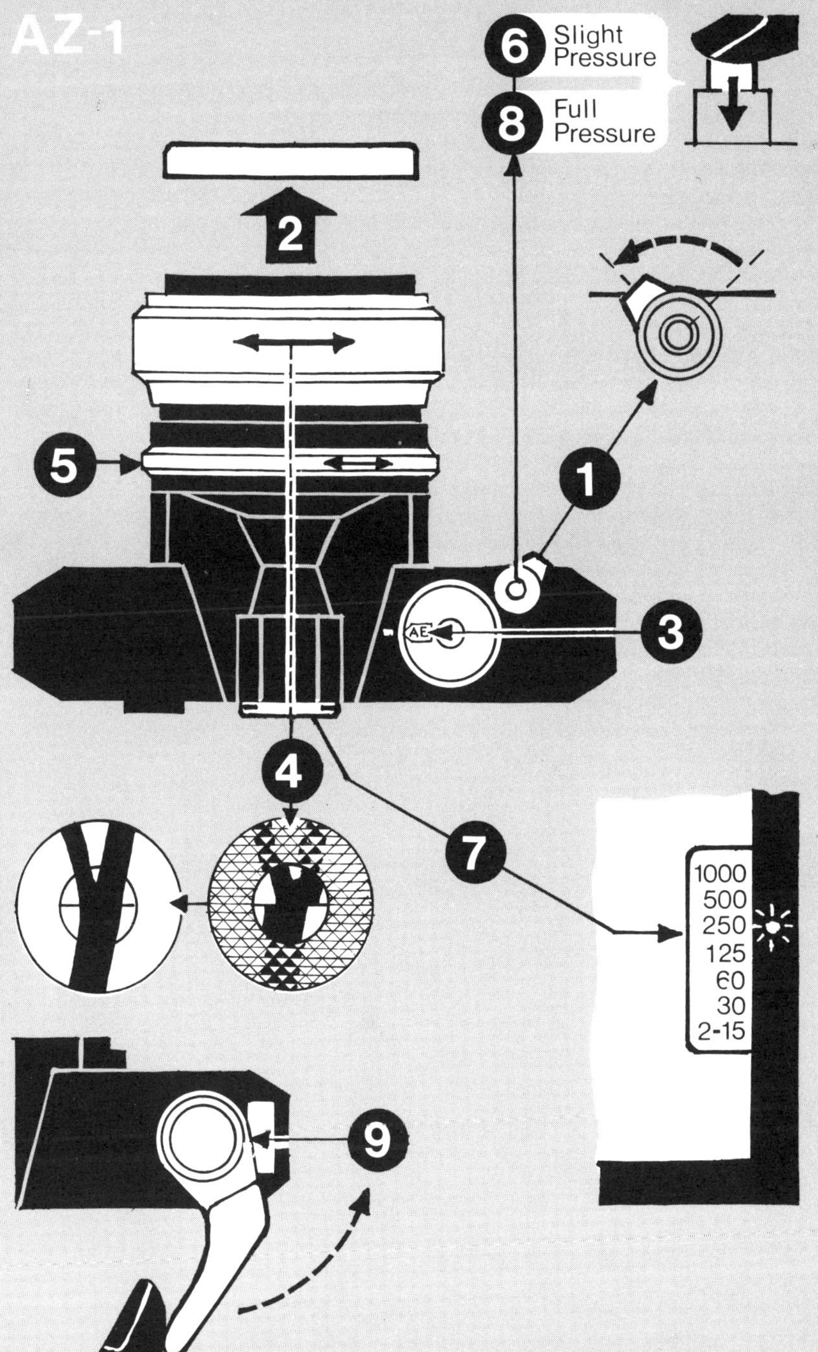
AZ-1
6 Slight Pressure
8 Full Pressure
2
5
1
AE
3
4
7
1000
500
250
125
60
30
2-15
9

Unloading the Fujica SLR cameras

If you forget to watch the frame counter, you know when you reach the end of the film because you feel extra tension on the film transport lever. Do not force it or you might drag the film end out of the cassette and then have to unload the camera in total darkness. Or you might tear the perforations and leave a little piece of film to work its way into the shutter.

Press the film release button in the camera base and, if it does not stay depressed, hold it in while you complete the film transport operation and allow the lever to return. The film release button should then stay depressed. Fold out the rewind crank and turn it in the direction of the arrow until you feel a sudden lessening of resistance as the film leaves the take-up spool. Remember that a full cassette contains 150 cm (5 ft) of film but do not hurry the rewinding or you may cause streaking on the film from static electrical charges.

When you feel the film leave the take-up spool, stop winding unless you wish to wind the film completely back into the cassette. You may prefer to leave the leader protruding in case the lips of the cassette are not completely light-tight. That should not apply to new cassettes. If you want to wind the film completely into the cassette, give two or three extra turns of the crank. Then, at least, you will not reload the film into the camera under the impression that it is unexposed.

When the film has left the take-up spool, you can open the camera back. Pull the rewind knob upward against spring pressure at the end of its travel. The lock is then released and you can open the back fully. With the rewind knob still up, remove the cassette and push the rewind knob back. Close the camera back and press it firmly until it clicks into the locked position. Operate the film transport lever and the film release button will pop out.

If you are now putting the camera away, remember the check that the shutter release is locked, except on the ST605, which has no lock.

Unloading procedure

1 Press rewind button and hold. **2** Rewind film. **3** Pull up rewind knob to release back latch. **4** Open camera back. **5** Remove cassette. **6** Push back rewind knob. **7** Close camera back.

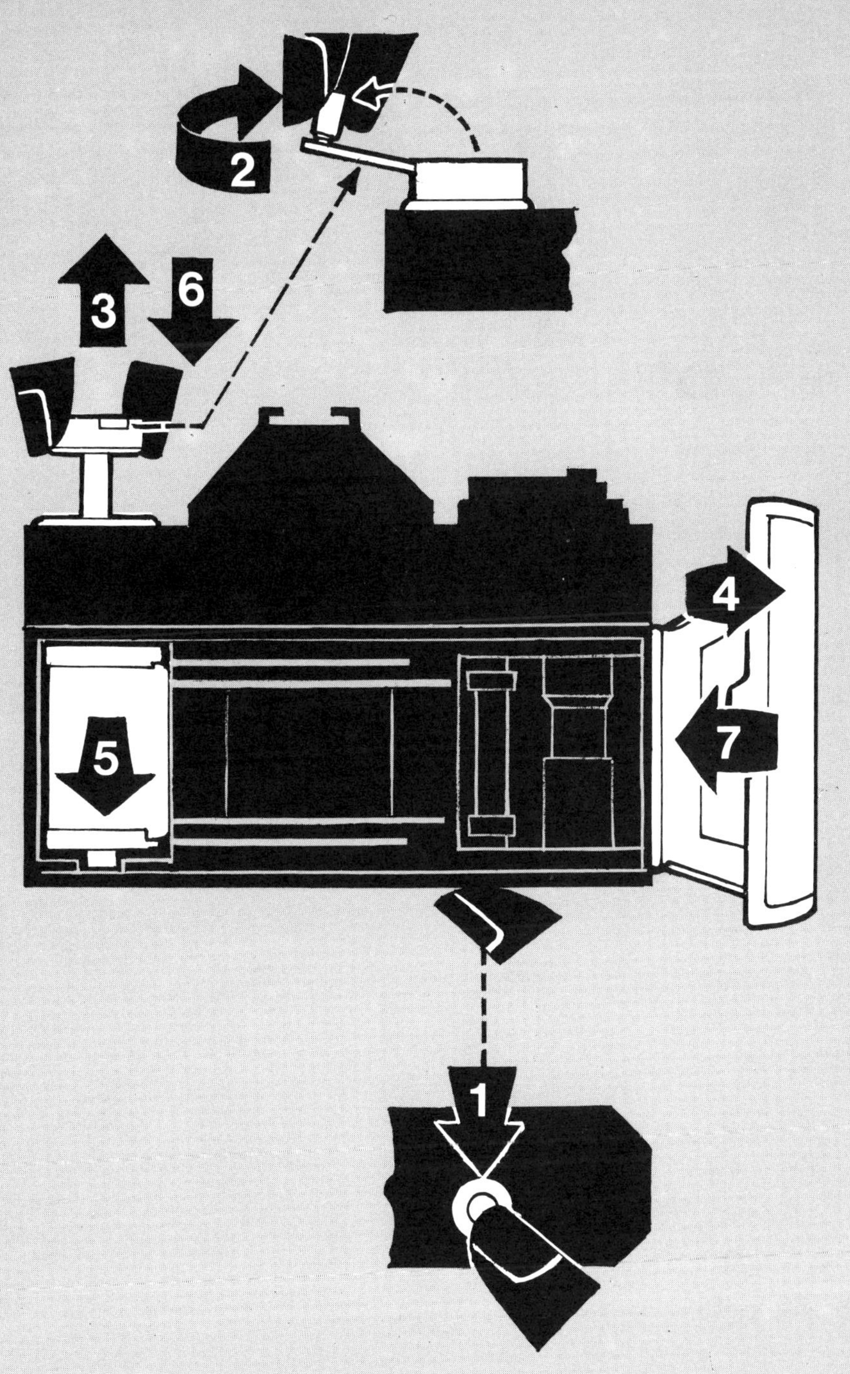
2
3
6
4
7
5
1

Flash synchronisation

The shutters of all the Fujica SLR cameras are X-synchronised for flash. This is the type of synchronisation designed primarily for electronic flash, which can be used at shutter speeds of 1/60 second and slower, including the B setting. Electronic flash units can be connected either to the contact in the accessory shoe (the hot shoe) if of the cordless type, or to the X contact on the camera front – the only contact in that position on the ST605 – if of the type with synchronisation cord.

The ST901 and AZ-1 can be used only at 1/60 second or on the B setting when set for manual operation because there are no manually-set slower speeds. It is normal to set these models to manual operation for flash work but it is possible to use electronic flash with the camera set to automatic if the indicated shutter speed is 1/30 second or slower. It is not advisable to use it if the indicated shutter speed is 1/60 second because the actual speed may be significantly faster.

The normal type of flashbulb (M or MF class) can also be used in units connected to either the X socket or the hot shoe, if appropriate, but only at shutter speeds of 1/15 second and slower, including the B setting. On the 901 and AZ–1, that means that they can be used only with the camera set for automatic operation and also really means that the camera is not particularly well suited to the use of flashbulbs.

FP synchronisation

An additional synchronisation socket is fitted to the camera front of all models except the ST605. This socket is marked FP on the ST models and is designed for use with special focal plane bulbs that have a longer than usual peak of illumination – more a plateau than a peak. They burn at full brilliance for a time sufficient for the gap between the blinds at faster shutter speeds to traverse the full width of the film. Theoretically, it should be possible for them to be used at all shutter speeds but Fuji specifically recommend that they be used for preference at 1/60 or 1/125 second and suggest that unsatisfactory results might be obtained at speeds faster than 1/500 second. Experiment is the only answer if you wish to use this type of flash. Results may vary from camera to camera. The AZ-1 socket is for X synchronisation only.

Flash synchronisation

The ST605 and AZ–1 are X-synchronised only, primarily for electronic flash. The other models have both X and FP synchronisation but the ST901 is essentially an automatic camera and not really suited to flashbulb use.

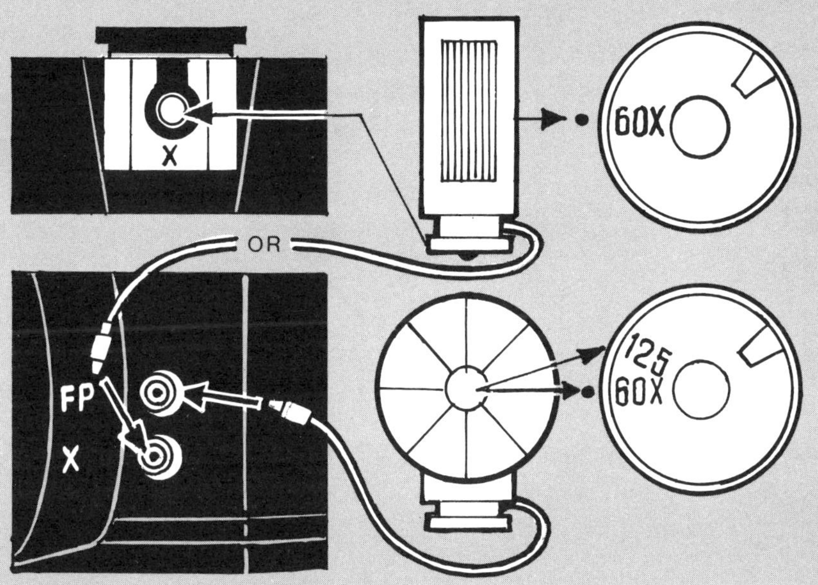
X
60X
OR
FP
X
125
60X
ST901,801,705

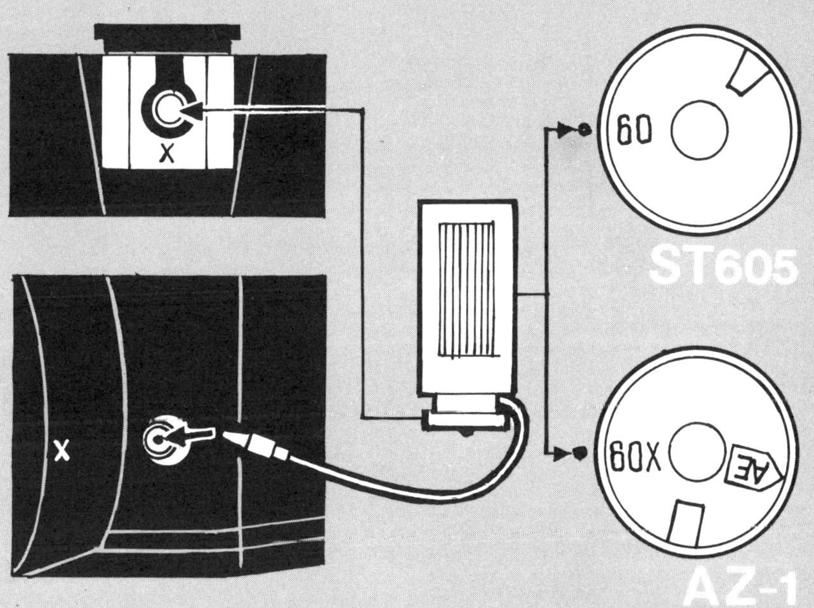
X
60
ST605
X
60X
AE
AZ-1

The colour pictures

Your Fujica is suitable for taking most types of picture. The single-lens reflex system allows you to see just what your pictures will look like whatever lens or accessory you fit.

People

People always make popular subjects, they can be carrying on any of a wide range of activities, or just looking glamorous. Commonly, they are pictured doing nothing in particular, and your main object is to produce a good likeness. There is still variety—you can take a formal portrait, or a candid snap from a distance. Give your subject something to do, playing in the waves for example, and you will add to the feeling of presence. The bright sun too, can produce a strong holiday atmosphere in sea-side shots. Be careful with its angle, though. Harsh shadows across her face can transform the most attractive model into something resembling a witch. Light surroundings though, reduce the harshness very greatly; and foaming sea is particularly good for that.

A little diffusion in the lighting is often available in woodland areas. As well as lightening the shadows, this makes their edges hazier; a particular advantage with photographs of children.

Go in close

Close shots of flowers, on the other hand benefit from strong lighting. The bright magenta of fuchsia bells makes them stand out starkly against a green background. Sidelighting is needed though, to show their shape. If directly from behind the camera, these delicate blooms would look like cut-outs hanging in the air.

Flash

Small objects in museums or other collections need to be recorded sharply and accurately. A small portable electronic flash is ideal for this. The reflector is large enough to produce a reasonably diffuse light in close shots. Held a little way away from the camera lens, the flash provides all the modelling necessary. It also illuminates the subject brightly and allows you to set a small aperture to give you enough depth of field. The poorly lit background forms a good backdrop.

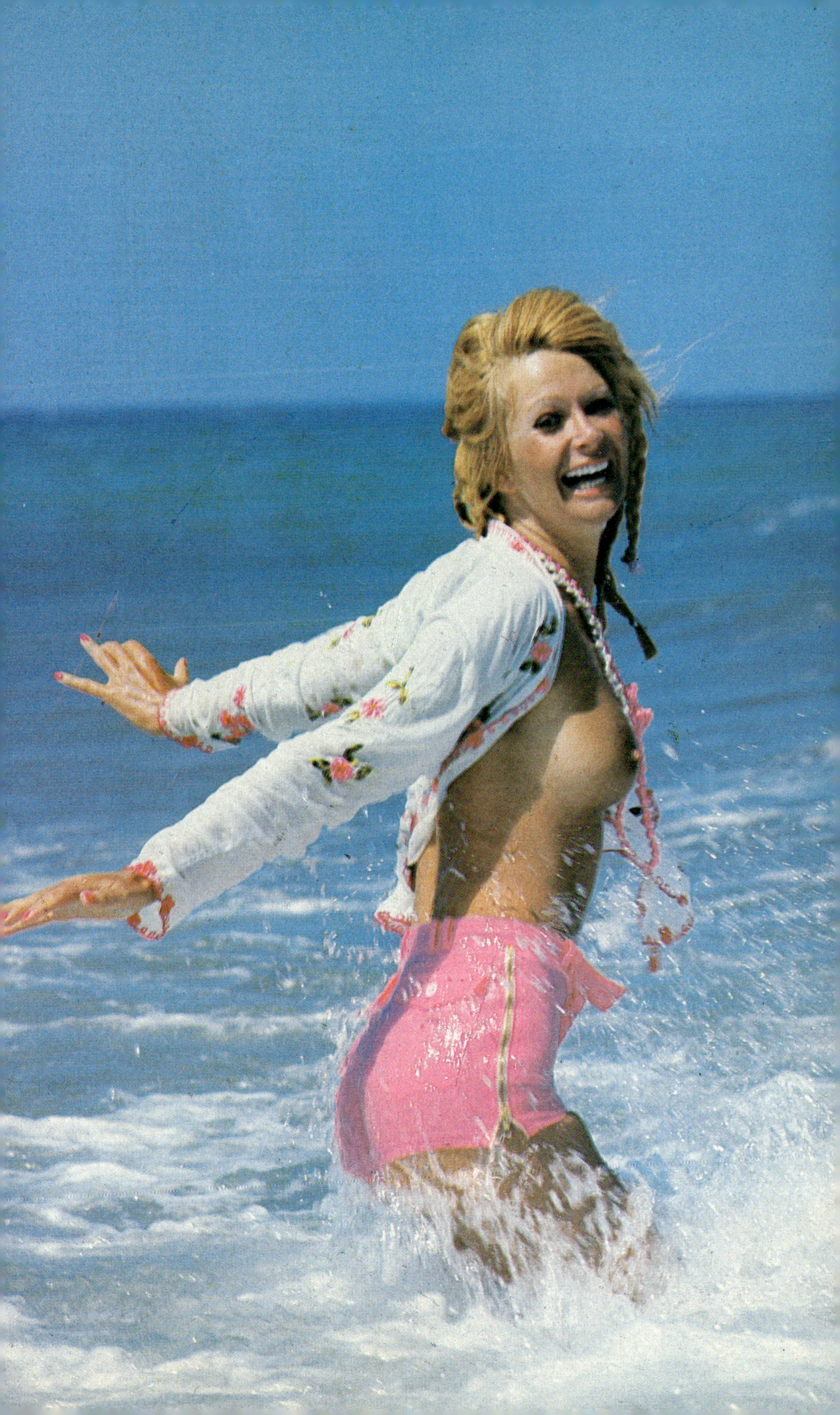

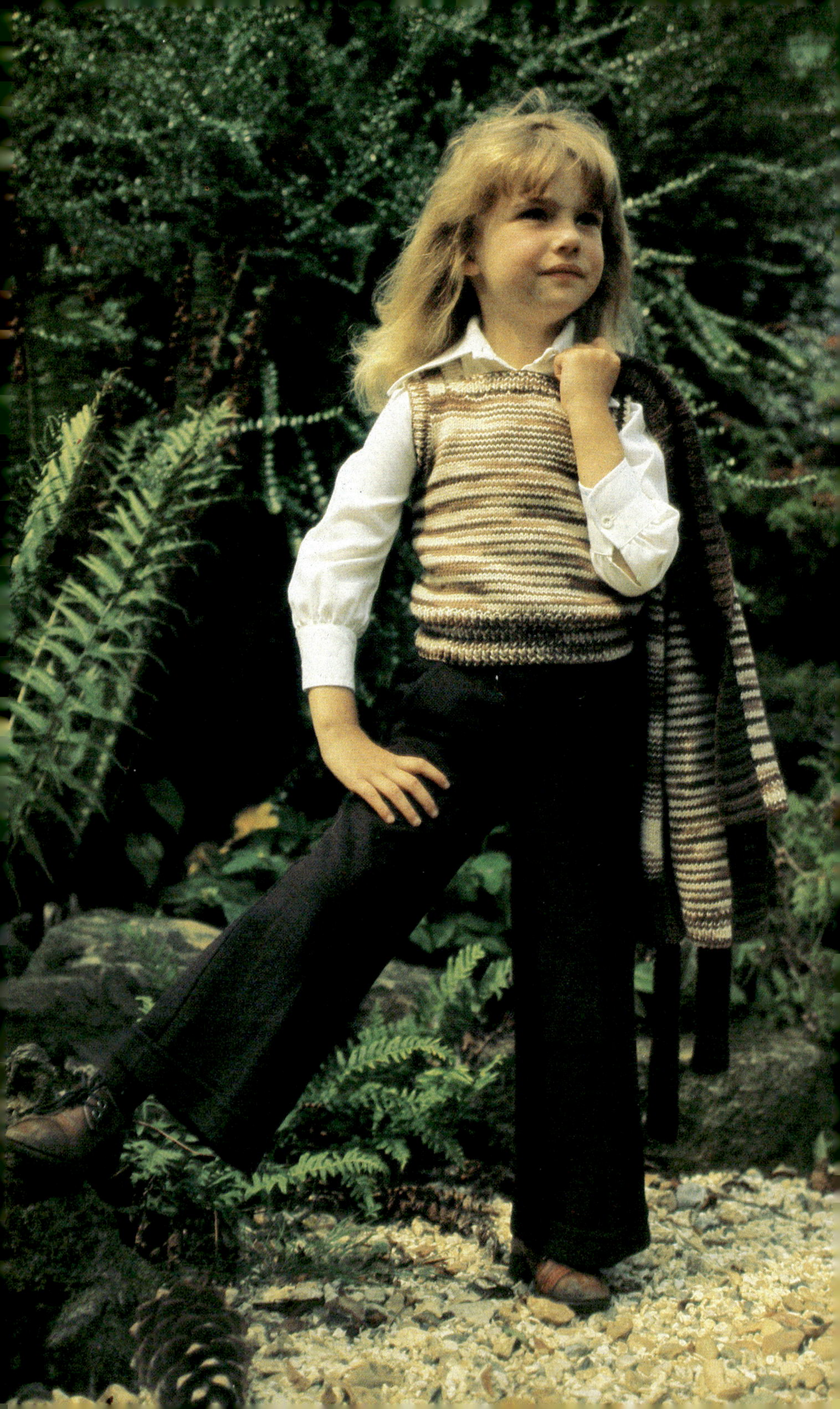

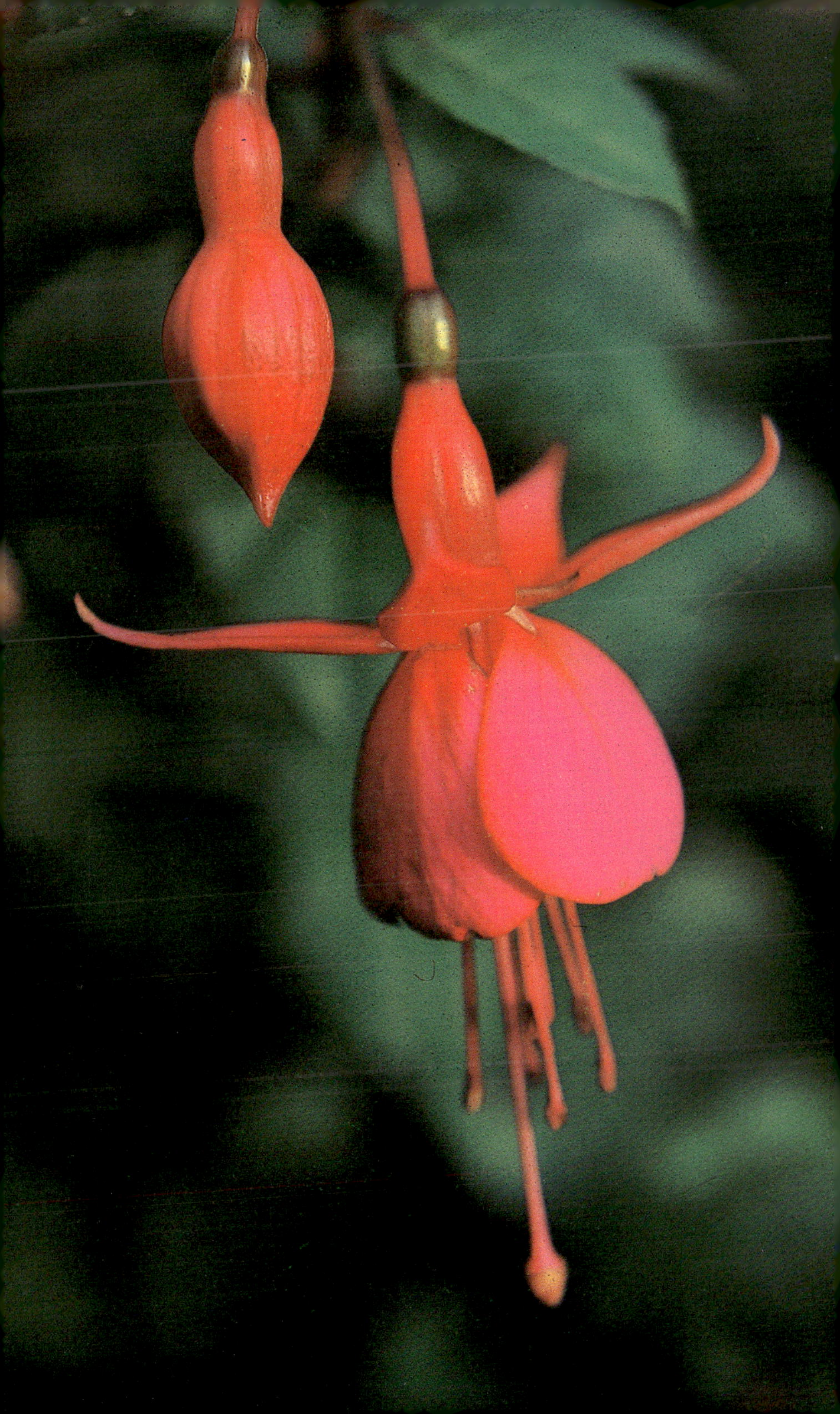

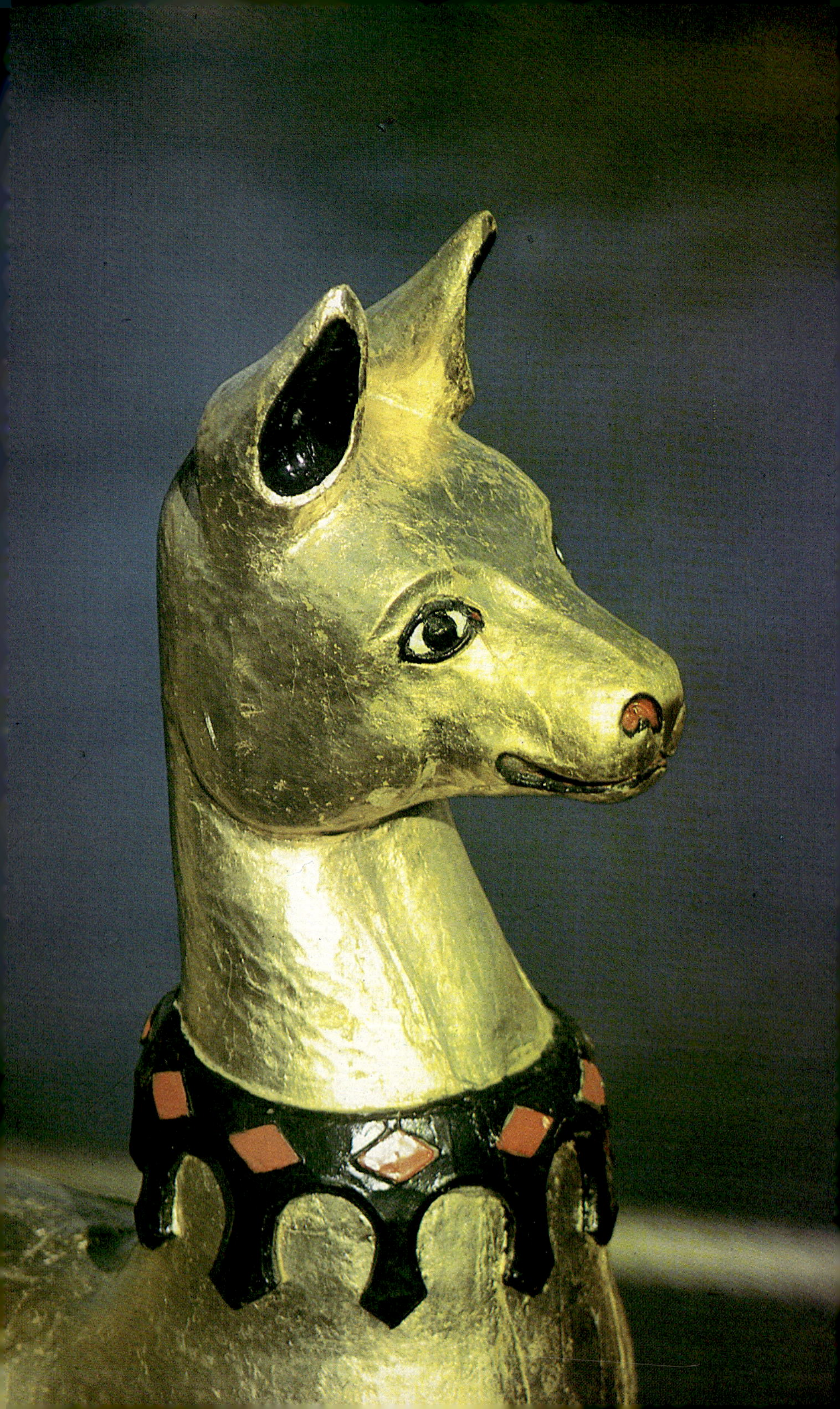

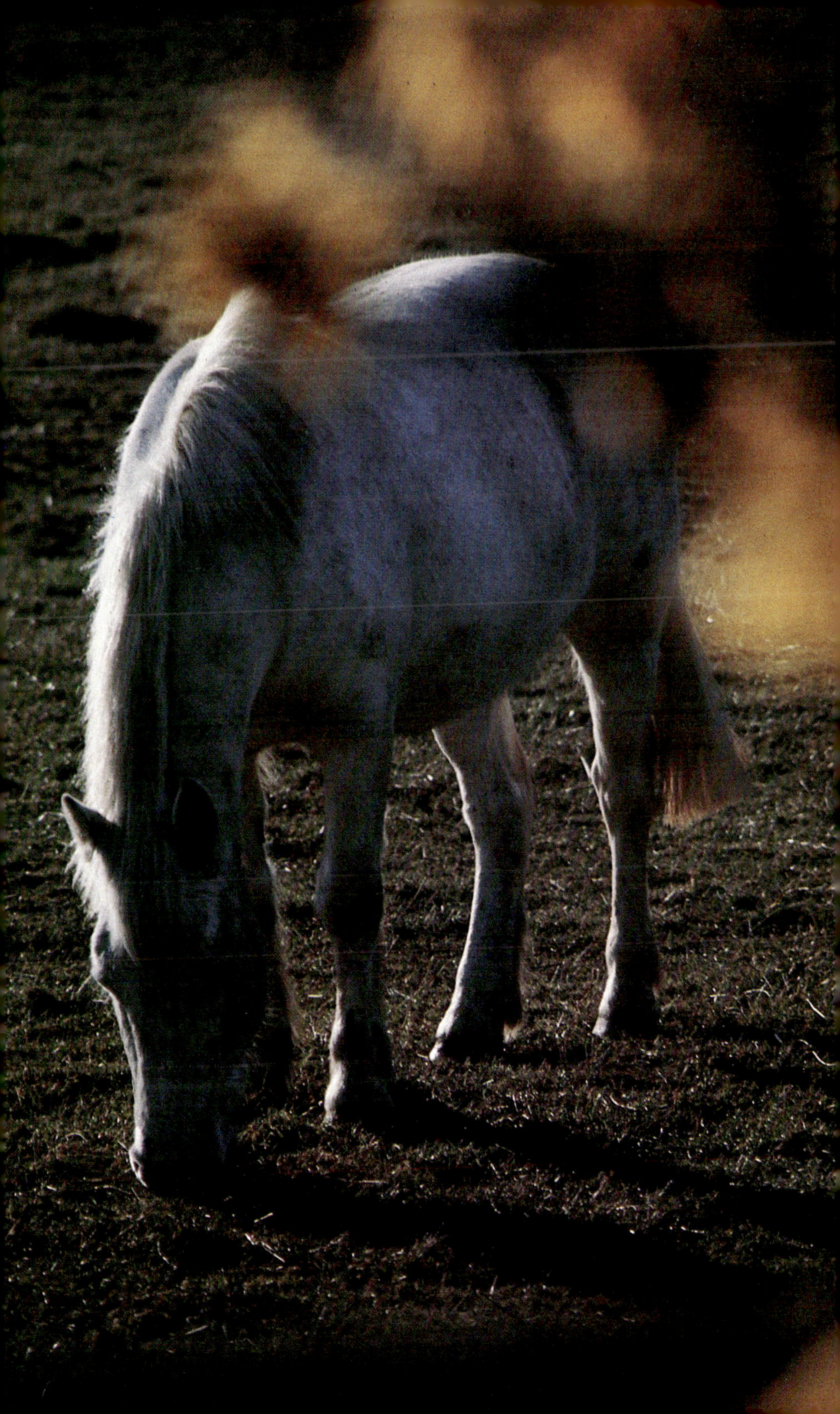

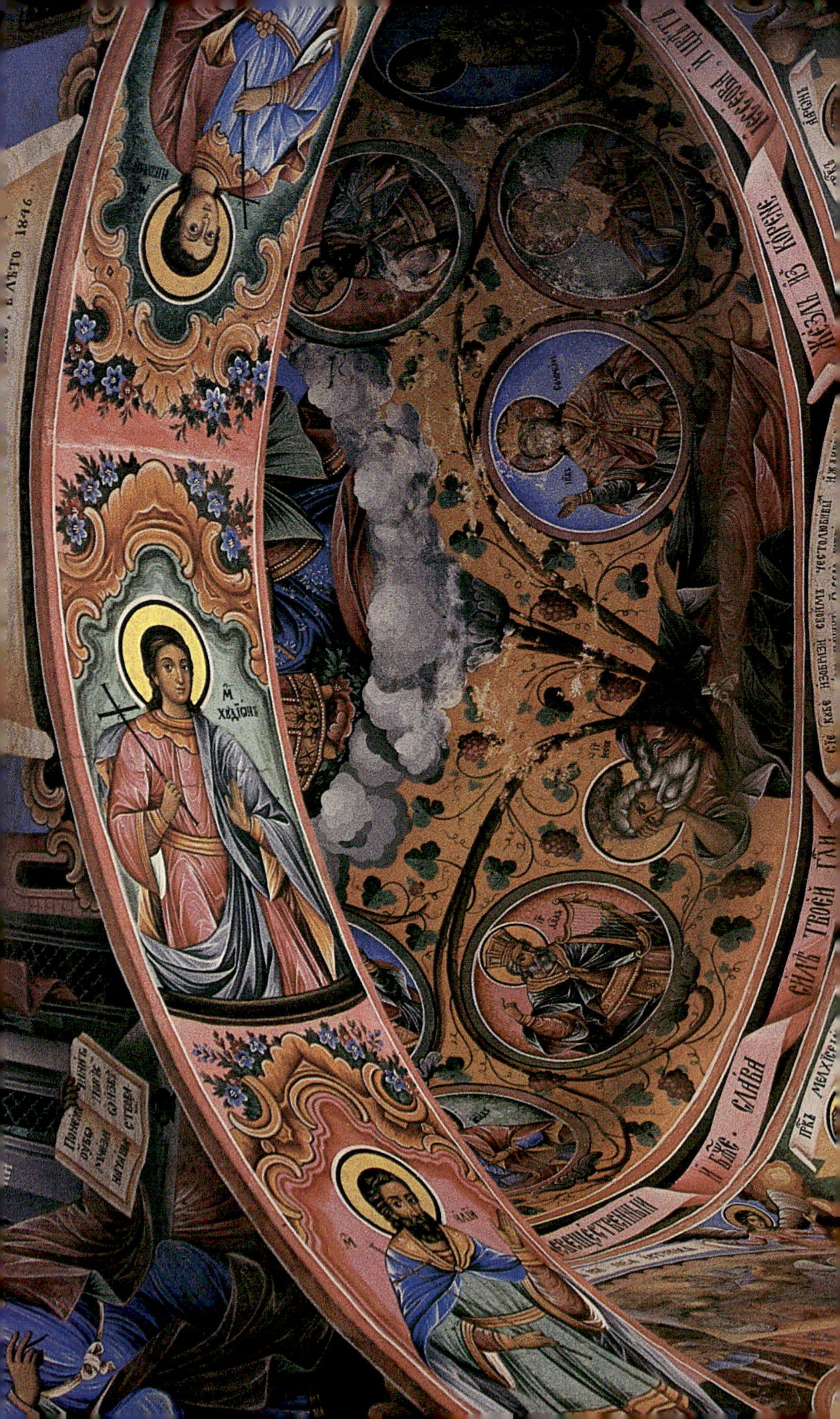

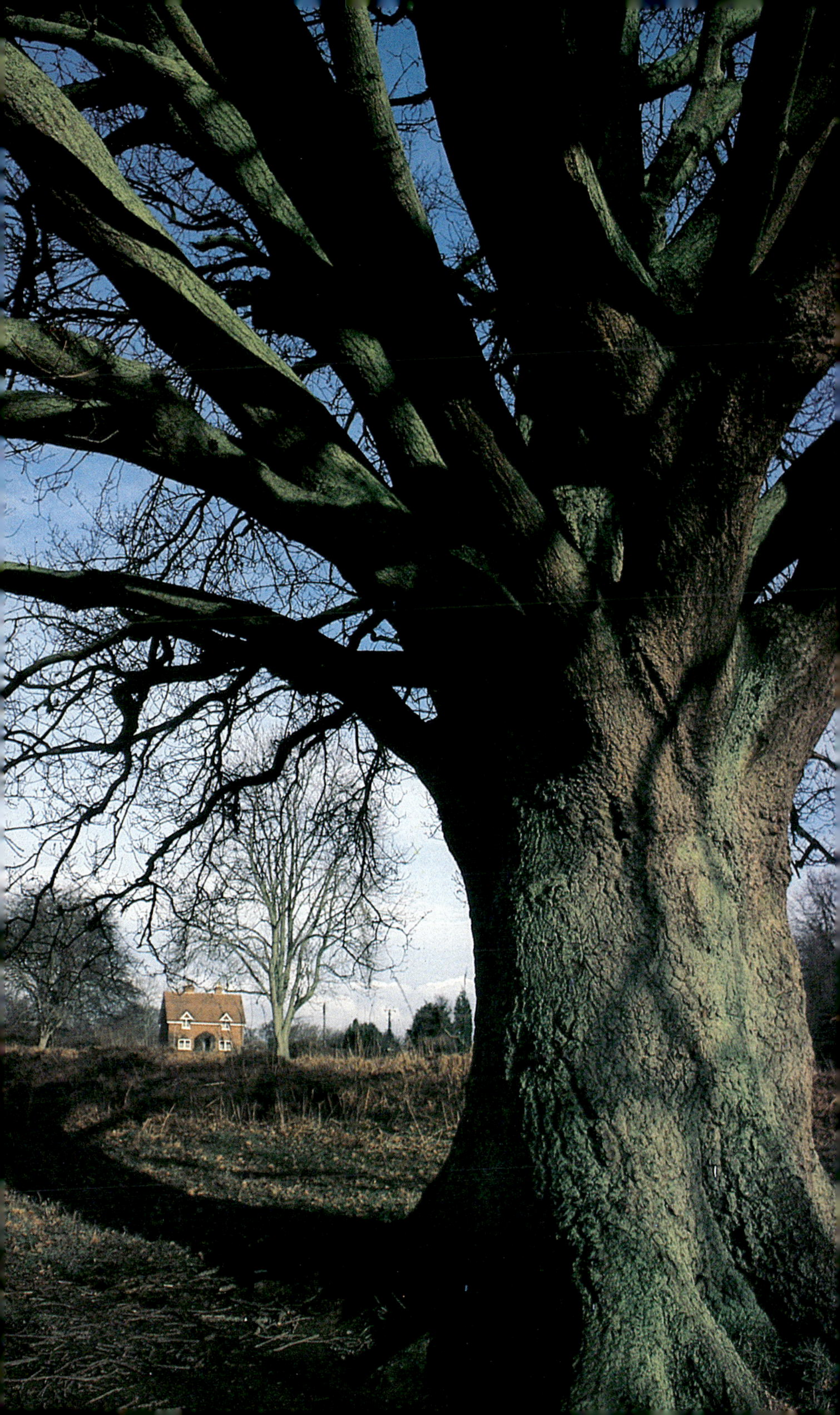

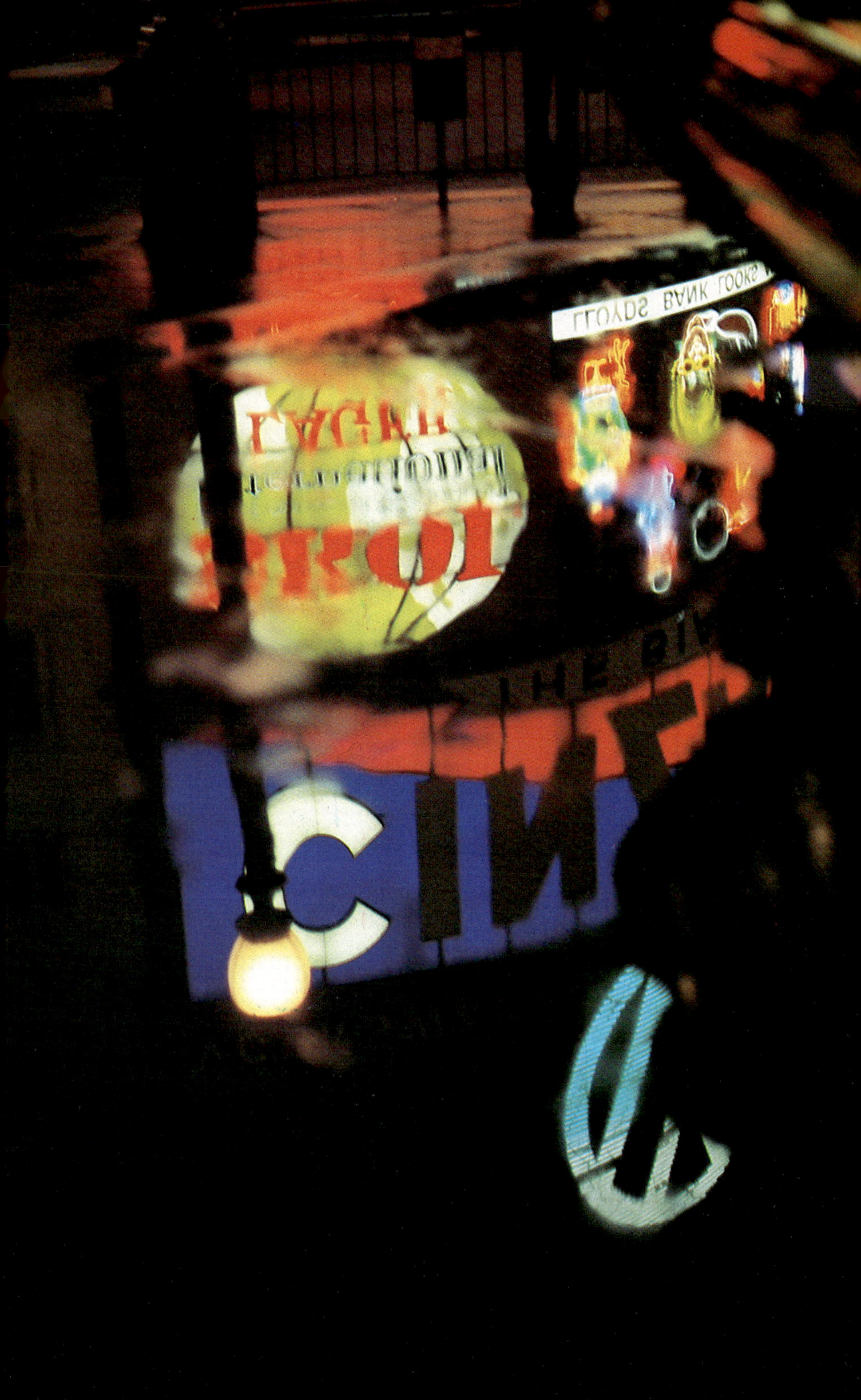

Animals

In the photographer's hierarchy, animals come closely behind people as suitable subjects. Often though, they can be treated in a sculptural way. Strong morning sunlight can outline a feeding horse with light creating an almost abstract picture; yet without losing the obvious horse shape. Exposure is critical for shots like this, and you are well advised to bracket your chosen combination into over- and underexposed pictures. This applies equally with manual and automatic exposure cameras.

Interiors

Indoors, the problem is not usually in deciding on the exposure, but in being able to choose a long enough shutter speed or wide enough lens aperture in the comparatively dim surroundings. Use a good strong tripod to hold your camera very steady. Then you can choose a long (time) exposure, and thus a small aperture so that everything comes out sharp.

Natural beauty

Out and about, whether in town or country, pictures are very much what you make them. They reflect, to a large extent, your personality and interests. The scene appeals to you, so you photograph it. Unfortunately, the resulting picture so often bears no resemblance to your appreciation of the original. The cause is usually lack of awareness on your part, often because you did not concentrate on the interesting aspects. A single tree, photographed from a carefully chosen viewpoint can evoke the atmosphere of a scene in the way that an overall shot possibly can not.

Look around

Don't just look at the obvious things. Look up, look down, everywhere. Pictures appear in the most unusual places. "The reflection of night lights in a roadside puddle" does not sound the recipe for success. But it can make you a sparkling and attractive picture.

Photographs by: Colin Ramsay p. 81, Peter Stiles pp. 82, 84 and 88, Raymond Lea pp. 83, 85 and 87 and J. Burt p. 86.

Flash exposures

Unlike other light sources, a flashbulb or single firing of an electronic flash tube emit a finite, constant and measurable amount of light. In general use the flash is also small enough to be regarded as a point light source, which means that it is subject to the inverse square law—the amount of light reaching the subject is in inverse proportion to the ratio between the squares of the flash-to-subject distances. With the flash at 9 ft the light on the subject is $(3/9)^2$ or one-ninth the strength of the same flash at 3 ft from the subject.

Lens apertures work in a similar way. At *f*2 the light transmitted is $(8/2)^2$ or 16 times the light transmitted at *f*8.

Thus, whenever flash distance and *f*-number multiplied together give the same result the amount of light reaching the film is the same, i.e. *f*2 and 20 ft, *f*4 and 10 ft, *f*8 and 5 ft etc., because, for example, changing from *f*4 to *f*2 *increases* light transmission fourfold while changing the flash distance from 10 ft to 20 ft *decreases* the light falling on the subject fourfold.

If these factors provided correct exposure, therefore the figure 40 could be ascribed to that particular flash unit as an exposure guide number.

That is how the guide number system works. Every flashbulb and electronic flash unit has guide numbers applicable to various film speeds. Flashbulb packings also quote different guide numbers according to shutter speed but these do not normally apply to focal plane shutters, with which the faster speeds cannot be used. You take the open flash or 1/30 sec number. When using focal plane type bulbs, you should use the guide number for your chosen shutter speed.

To calculate the aperture required for correct exposure, you simply divide the flash distance (not the camera distance, unless the flash is on the camera) into the guide number and round off to the nearest *f*-number. Alternatively, if you wish to shoot at a particular aperture you divide the *f*-number into the guide number to find the distance at which you have to place the flash.

If that means that the flash has to be used at a greater distance than that from which you wish to shoot, you can use an extension flash cable, obtainable from any photo dealer.

Typical flash guide numbers (feet/metres)

Flash source	Film speeds (ASA) 25–40	50–80	100–160	200–320	400–640
MF Class bulbs					
Small bulbs, magicubes flashcubes (Type 1B, AG1B, AG3B etc)	60/18	80/24	120/36	160/48	240/72
Medium (Type 5B etc)	100/30	160/48	200/60	320/96	400/120
FP-Class bulbs					
Medium (Type 6B etc)	45/14	65/20	90/27	130/39	180/54
Electronic flash					
Small pocket guns	25/8	40/12	50/15	80/24	100/30
Medium pocket guns	40/12	60/18	80/24	120/36	160/48
Large 'pocket' guns	50/15	70/21	100/30	140/142	200/60
'Professional' type guns	70/21	100/30	140/42	200/60	280/76

Guide numbers for bulbs apply only to shutter speeds of 1/30 second or longer (1/60 with FP bulbs). At shorter speeds the number must be reduced.
Electronic flash guide numbers apply at all suitable speeds.

Using flash

Many modern cameras have an accessory shoe mounted on the pentaprism with a centre flash contact. A cableless flashgun can fit directly into the shoe and make contact with the flash switch linked to the shutter blind movement. Cameras with no built-in accessory shoe can usually be fitted with an attachable type. The flashgun is then plugged in to the appropriate flash socket on the camera.

A flashgun on the camera does not, however, provide a very satisfactory lighting arrangement. It throws harsh shadows on nearby backgrounds and possibly under the nose, chin, hairline, etc. according to the camera position. It provides little or no modelling to features.

A simple solution to these problems is to tilt the flashgun upward or sideways to reflect light back on to the subject from a large surface, which must be white or neutral-coloured if you use colour film. Special accessories for tilting camera-mounted flash units can be obtained from photo dealers.

Whenever possible, it is better to remove the flash unit from the camera and place it to one side on an extension lead. This serves the dual purpose of separating the shadow from the subject, perhaps allowing it to be excluded from the picture area, and at the same time giving some modelling to the features by a greater variation of light and shade.

Using a second flash

Even when off the camera, however, the single flash still throws heavy shadows and, when placed for the best modelling effect, may leave parts of the subject in almost complete shadow. Such shadows can be relieved by placing a reflecting surface, such as a large card, on the other side of the subject so as to throw light back on to it or by using a second flashgun or extension head, where available, at the camera position.

The second flash should be weaker than that used for modelling because its function is to lighten the shadows slightly, not to obliterate them. It should, therefore, be farther away than the main light or should be covered by a layer or two of clean handkerchief. The second flash (plugged into a Y-connector) should preferably be of the same make and model as the first, and the method is not fully recommended owing to the possibility of overloading the flash contacts in the camera. Flash manufacturers can usually supply slave sensors which give the second flash automatically on receiving light from the first.

Flash can also be used as a fill-light in daylight, particularly to relieve the shadows thrown by an unclouded sun. You should preferably take your subject into the shade but where that is not possible, shadows thrown by back or side lighting from the sun can be relieved by a weak frontal flash. When using flash in this way, the guide number for exposure purposes should be at least doubled.

The guide number has to be modified for bounced flash too. The effective flash distance is from flash to reflecting surface and thence to the subject. There may be losses by absorption at the reflecting surface, but these are generally offset by some direct light reaching the subject from the edge of the flash beam.

Where two flashguns or an extension head are used, it is not usually necessary to take any account for exposure of the fill-in flash.

Using and changing EBC Fujinon lenses

Lenses are attached to the Fujica cameras by a simple screw thread. All you do is to rotate the whole lens to screw it into or out of the camera body. The thread is the so-called "universal" 42 mm type originally introduced for the Praktica cameras and subsequently adopted by many other manufacturers.

Full-aperture metering system

As all the Fujicas except the 605 are full-aperture metering cameras, however, there is a slight additional complication. Around the lens mounting ring on the camera body, there is a further ring that rotates clockwise against a light spring pressure. The extent to which it is turned indicates to the meter circuit the setting of the aperture control ring on the lens. The farther it turns in a clock-wise direction, the greater the aperture that is pre-set on the lens. Thus, it does not matter that different lenses have different maximum apertures because the ring on the camera body has a small stud that is turned by a lug on the aperture control ring on the lens. The position of that lug varies with the maximum aperture of the lens.

The movement of the aperture teller ring has to be precise, so the lens flange on the camera body has a small sprung stud in about the eight o'clock position that slips into a recess in the rear of the lens as the screw thread is tightened. Thus, the lens always locates in exactly the same position.

Apart from the small lug and recess on the back of Fujinon lenses, they look much like any other screw thread automatic diaphragm lens. They have only a spring pin that closes down the lens diaphragm to its pre-set value when pushed by a mechanism in the camera body connected to the shutter release and the stop-down button.

Lens changing

To remove a Fujinon lens from the camera (except the ST605), you press the lens lock release on the mirror box next to the self-timer and turn the lens anticlockwise. It separates from the body in about $2\frac{1}{2}$ turns. To attach a lens, you simply screw it in. A Fujinon lens locks into position with a click. Any other 42 mm screw thread lens tightens to the end of the thread.

Almost any 42 mm lens from other manufacturers can be used on the Fujica STs but it is advisable to check older lenses to ensure that the internal barrel does not protrude significantly beyond the end of the thread or it may foul the mirror. Take care if you use a Praktica electric lens because the electrical contacts foul the locking stud on the Fujica as you tighten the lens. You can clear it, however, by pressing the lens lock release and continuing to tighten.

Lenses other than the Fujinons or those made specifically for the Fujicas will generally operate normally in all respects except full-aperture metering. As they have no lock or aperture-teller lug, they must be used for stop-down metering only.

Lens changing

A Remove lens by depressing lens lock release (except on ST605) and turning lens anticlockwise. **B 1** Lens lock release. **2** Aperture teller. **3** Lens lock. **4** Auto diaphragm mechanism. **C** Replace lens by screwing in clockwise.

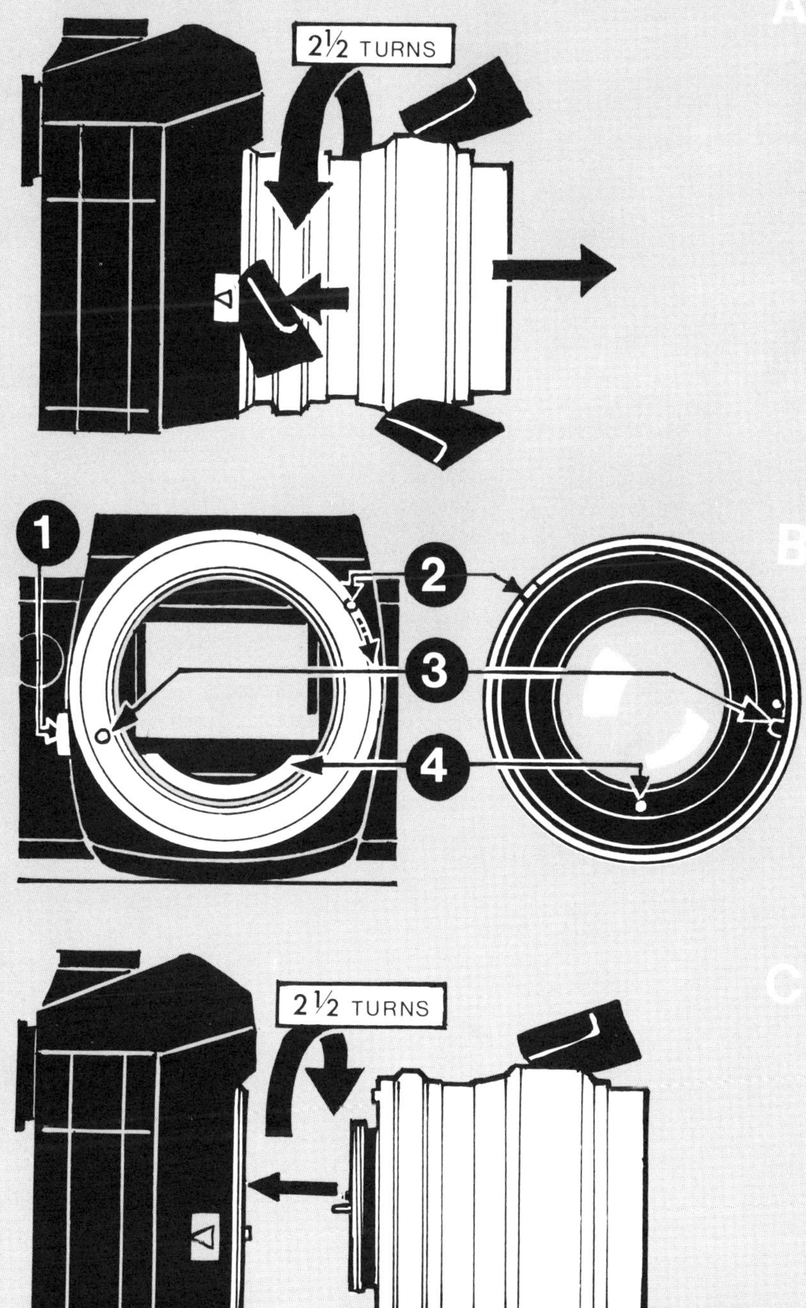
A
2½ TURNS
B
1
2
3
4
C
2½ TURNS

Wide-angle and standard lenses

The shorter the focal length of a lens, the wider its angle of view. The Fujinon lenses range from a 16 mm fisheye type with an angle of view of 180 degrees to a 1000 mm taking in an arc of no more than 2½ degrees. So the fisheye takes in virtually everything in front of it on a much reduced scale, while the 1000 mm has extreme tunnel vision and magnifies the scale of objects within its vision beyond the capability of the human eye. Between the two, there are more moderately wide-angle lenses, so-called standard or normal focal length lenses and less extreme long-focus types.

Fisheye lens

Wide-angle lenses are becoming more popular as they become less difficult to make. They used to have tendencies toward vignetting (a lack of illumination in the corners of the image) and barrel distortion (an outward curvature of straight lines). The latter distortion is still evident, of course, in a fisheye lens. Indeed, it is left uncorrected in order to obtain the 180 degree angle, which would be impossible without it. The Fujinon fisheye, however, is of the type providing 180 degree coverage on the image diagonal only, so that the whole image area is used. Those giving full 180-degree coverage produce a circular image within the frame.

Wide-angle lenses such as the 28 and 35 mm are useful for those who shoot habitually in cramped surroundings or who wish to have sufficient depth of field at relatively close range to be able to shoot quickly and confidently without constant refocusing. They are often also valuable, either for practical purposes or special effects, in providing great apparent disparity of size between foreground and background.

The standard focal length for 35 mm work is generally conceded to be about 50 mm because, at the theoretically correct viewing distance, such a lens gives a perspective effect that seems about normal to the human eye. In this range, Fuji have 50 mm and 55 mm lenses and a special 55 mm macro type (see page 102).

Angles of view

The wide-angle and standard lenses range from the 180-deg angle of the 16mm fisheye to about 42-deg for the 55mm.

EBC Fujinon wide-angle and standard lenses

Focal length (mm)	Angle (°)	Aperture max	min	Min. focus m	ft	Filter size mm	Length mm	in	Weight g	oz
16	180	2.8	22	0.25	0.8	built in	55.5	2.2	425	15
19	96	3.5	22	0.3	1.0	77	48	1.9	264	9.3
28	74	3.5	16	0.4	1.3	49	38.5	1.5	184	6.5
35	62.7	1.9	16	0.4	1.3	49	48	1.9	230	8
35	62.7	2.8	16	0.4	1.3	49	44	1.7	185	6.5
50	45.4	1.4	16	0.45	1.5	49	43.5	1.7	270	9.5
55	42.2	1.8	16	0.45	1.5	49	42	1.6	200	7
55	42.2	3.5	32	0.24	0.8	49	51.5	2	205	7.2

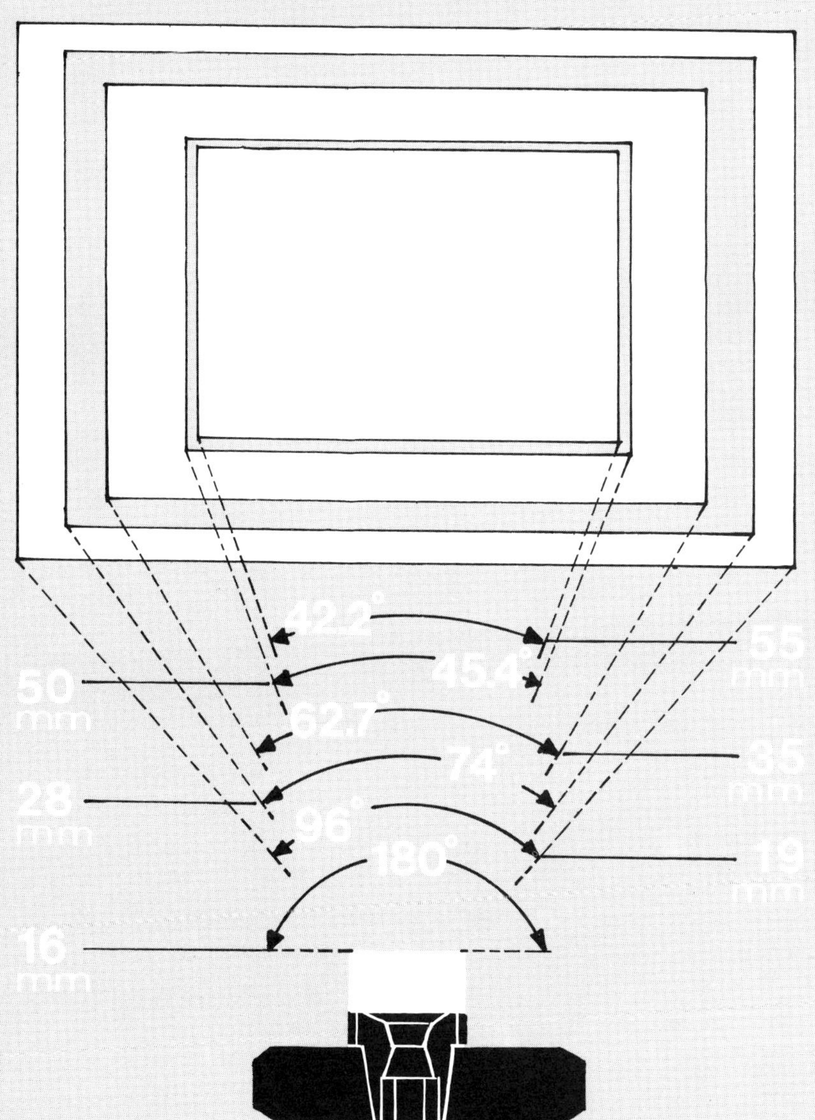
42.2°
55 mm
45.4°
50 mm
62.7°
35 mm
74°
28 mm
96°
19 mm
180°
16 mm

Long-focus lenses

All the Fujinon long-focus lenses are of telephoto construction. This means they are more compact than might be expected. Even the 1000 mm lens is only 715 mm (28 in) long. "Only" is a comparative term, of course. It is short compared with its focal length, but a lens more than 2 ft long and weighing about 11 lb is not easy to handle. It needs a stout tripod on a firm foundation to provide the quality image of which it is capable.

This is true of most long-focus lenses. Although it is tempting to try long range shots of almost invisible subjects, you have little hope of seeing much on the film unless the camera is kept really still at the moment of exposure. Even then, at extremely long range you need clear air to shoot through.

Mounting unit

The longer-focus Fujinon lenses (400 mm upward) have a tripod mounting ring and a camera mounting tube. You first mount the lens on the tripod then turn the ring behind the focusing index to bring its white dot to the top, in line with the mounting unit dot and the focusing index. Pull the mounting unit off the lens and screw it into the camera body. Attach camera and mounting unit to lens by again lining up the three marks, pushing the mounting unit in and twisting the ring in front of it to the right to lock it. Keep the unit pressed in hard while you turn the locking ring and make sure that it locks properly. The mounting ring will not go into the lens if the locking ring has meanwhile been turned to the right. Turn it at least a complete turn to the left to line up the dots.

The shorter Fujinon long-focus lenses provide a useful magnification and can be hand held with reasonable care. The 200 mm *f*4.5, at only a little over 5 in long and one pound in weight, gives an image four times greater than that from the standard 50 mm lens and is not too difficult to hold steady. As lenses become more compact, the 200 mm is gradually replacing the 135 mm as first choice in the long-focus range. The shorter focal length still has the advantage of greater speed, however, while those who use a wide-angle as standard are also catered for by a 100 mm lens in the Fujinon range.

Soft-focus lens

A 100 mm lens is generally very good for portraiture but Fuji are producing a special lens in the field. The 85 mm *f*4 has a slightly longer than standard focal length with an inbuilt degree of controllable soft focus.

Angles of view

The range of long focus lenses runs from 85mm to 1000mm with angles of view from 28 to 2.5 deg.

EBC Fujinon long-focus lenses

Focal length	Angle (°)	Aperture max	Aperture min	Min. focus m	Min. focus ft	Filter mm	Length mm	Length in	Weight g	Weight oz
85	28.6	4	16	1	3.3	49	64.5	2.5	285	10
100	24.4	2.8	22	1.2	4	49	60	2.4	254	9
135	18	2.5	22	1.5	5	58	80	3.1	432	15.2
135	18	3.5	22	1.5	5	49	79	3.1	300	10.6
200	12.3	4.5	22	3.5	8	49	133	5.2	489	17.2
400	6.2	4.5	45	8	26	49	289	11.4	1925	68
600	4	5.6	45	12.5	41	49	410	17.3	3000	106
1000	2.5	8	45	30	98	49	715	28	4960	175

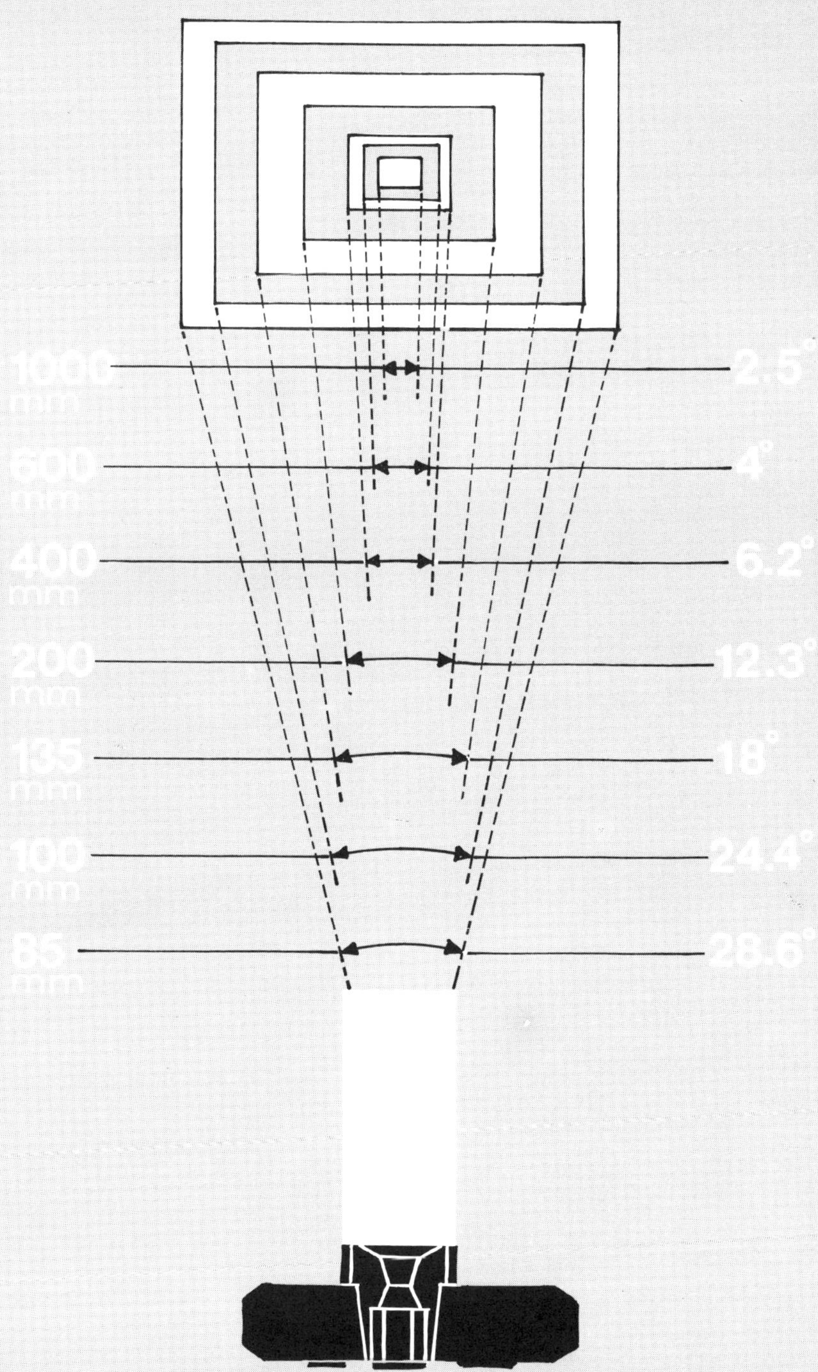

1000 mm
2.5°
600 mm
4°
400 mm
6.2°
200 mm
12.3°
135 mm
18°
100 mm
24.4°
85 mm
28.6°

EBC Fujinon zoom lenses

There is still a great deal of discussion about the merits and advantages of zoom lenses. They used to be difficult to make without some sacrifice of quality compared with lenses of a single focal length. The ability to maintain focus throughout the range of focal lengths provided was also suspect. These suspicions must still remain, particularly as regards the quality of the image. Sharpness is now usually more than adequate but it is not uncommon to find barrel or pincushion distortion more apparent in a zoom than in a prime lens.

The advantage of the zoom in versatility is undisputed but you have to accept a restriction on maximum aperture and minimum focusing distance and a not inconsiderable bulk. The Fujinon 54–270 mm lens, for example, is a remarkable achievement but at the short end it is a standard lens with a maximum *f*4.5 aperture, 2.5 m (6 ft) minimum focus and a weight of about $3\frac{1}{4}$ lb. Even at the long end, its 70 mm extra focal length compared with the 200 mm *f*4.5 costs 90 mm in length and more than 2 lb in weight.

The 75–150 mm is more manageable and provides a useful range of focal lengths at about half the weight of its bigger brother.

It is in zoom lenses and other multi-element lenses that Fuji's electron beam coating (EBC) is so valuable. Multi-coating has attracted a great deal of attention in recent years although it has been standard practice on specialist lenses (particularly for television) for a considerable time. The advantage with most lenses is minimal but when you have 15 glass elements in 12 groups, as you have in the Fujinon 54–270 mm zoom, losses by internal reflection would be significant without specialised coating techniques such as the Fuji EBC system. Key elements are coated with up to 11 layers of special materials to reduce reflections from their surfaces and thus to improve picture sharpness and colour balance. Flare, causing subdued colours and even colour distortion can be significantly reduced by these methods. Exceptionally, the 7-element 43-75 mm zoom is not multicoated.

Angles of view

Zoom lenses have the advantage of continuously variable angles of view.

EBC Fujinon zoom lenses

Focal length (mm) min	Focal length (mm) max	Angle (°) max	Angle (°) min	Aperture max	Aperture min	Min. focus m	Min. focus ft	Filter size mm	Length mm	Length in	Weight g	Weight oz
43	75	53	32	3.5	22	1.2	4	49	58	2.3	315	11.1
75	150	32	16.4	4.5	22	1.8	6	62	143	5.6	748	26.4
75	205	32	12.3	3.8	22	2	6.6	62	180	7.7	925	32.7
54	270	43.7	9.2	4.5	22	2.5	8	82	220	8.7	1464	51.6

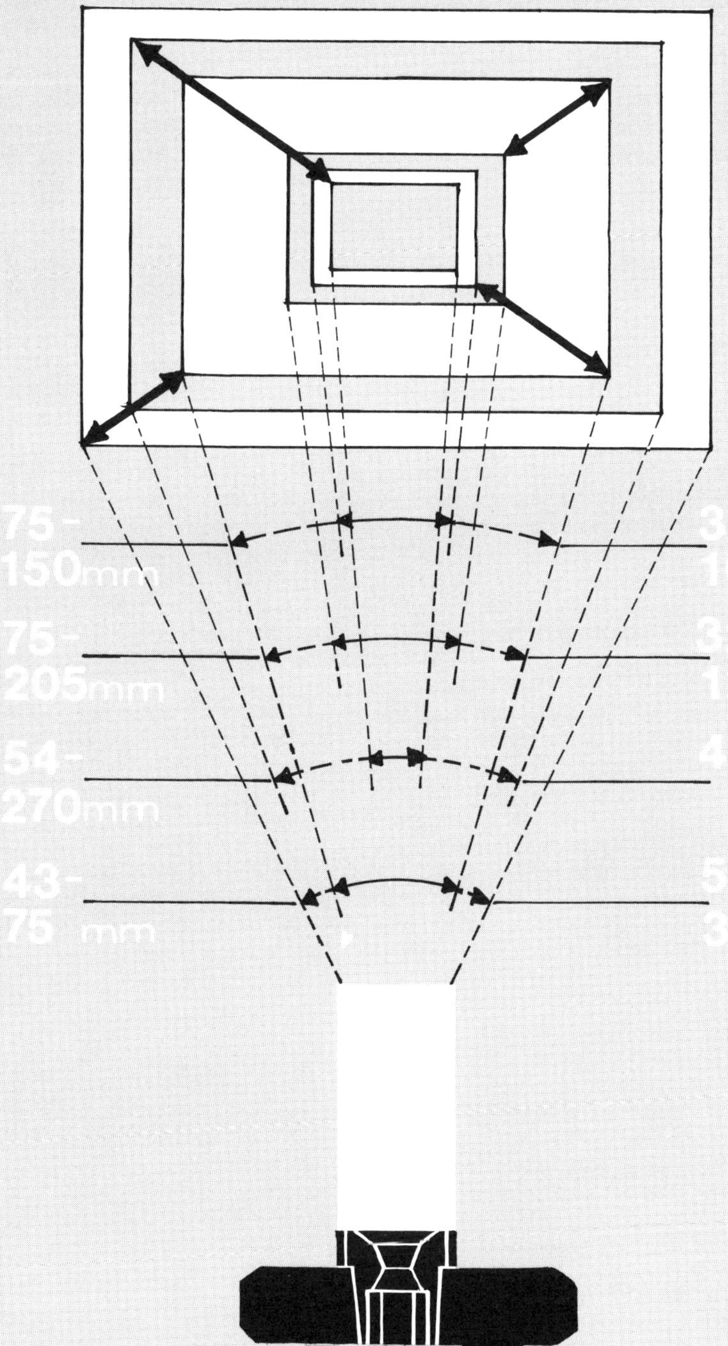

75-
150mm
32°
16.4°
75-
205mm
32°
12.3°
54-
270mm
43.6°
9.1°
43-
75 mm
53.3°
32°

Taking inexpensive close-ups

One of the great advantages of the single-lens-reflex design is that it allows you to get really close to your subject with the absolute minimum of equipment. When the camera lens is positioned one focal length from the film, it focuses distant objects. To focus closer, you move the lens farther away from the film. There is, though, a limit to the travel that can be built in to a lens mount.

Extension tubes

It is a simple matter on the other hand, to take the lens off the camera and put in a spacer tube to increase the separation between lens and film. Fuji supply a set of three such tubes, known as extension tubes, in 9.5, 19 and 28.5 mm lengths. There are also many types available from independent manufacturers. The tubes can be used with any lens but a given tube length provides greater magnification when used with a lens of shorter focal length. Using all three tubes behind a 55 mm lens, you can obtain a magnification of 1.18 (a little more than life size). With a 35 mm lens, magnification reaches 1.72. With a 135 mm, it is only 0.53.

The tubes have automatic diaphragm mechanisms but no aperture teller. Metering has to be carried out in the stopped-down mode on all models. You will find that added extension means extra exposure, and a less bright viewfinder image.

Close-up lenses

Although extension tubes provide a simple means of working at close range, there is a still simpler method. It does not call for extra exposure and therefore often allows you to use relatively fast shutter speeds. This method uses close-up or supplementary lenses.

Fuji supply only one close-up lens, allowing you to focus from about 11 in out to 19 in from the front of the close-up lens when you attach it to a camera lens. The focal length of the camera lens does not affect the focused distance but it does affect the image size in the normal way.

Close-up lenses are generally supplied in filter mounts that screw into the front of the lens. As most Fujinon lenses have the popular 49 mm thread, you can easily obtain close-up lenses of various strengths to allow you to shoot at really close range.

The quality obtainable with close-up lenses is surprisingly good but they are simple lenses and it is advisable to stop the camera lens down as far as possible to avoid using the marginal rays and to increase depth of field. Full-aperture metering can be carried out in the normal way.

Avoiding camera movement

With all close-range work, the camera must be rigidly supported because focusing is critical and depth of field is limited – even at very small apertures. Use a tripod or other firm support and a cable release to operate the shutter. As an alternative to the cable release, for static subjects, you can use the self-timer to allow camera vibrations to settle before the shutter is released. As very long exposures are set automatically on the ST901, an eyepiece shutter is fitted to prevent light entering the eyepiece and possibly affecting the exposure. The shutter is operated by a small lever to the left of the viewfinder eyepiece.

Simple close-ups

A The Fuji extension tubes are in a set of 9.5mm (No 1), 19mm (No 2) and 28.5mm (No 3). **B** Close-up lenses are generally supplied in powers of 1, 2 and 3 dioptres, giving progressively larger images from closer range.

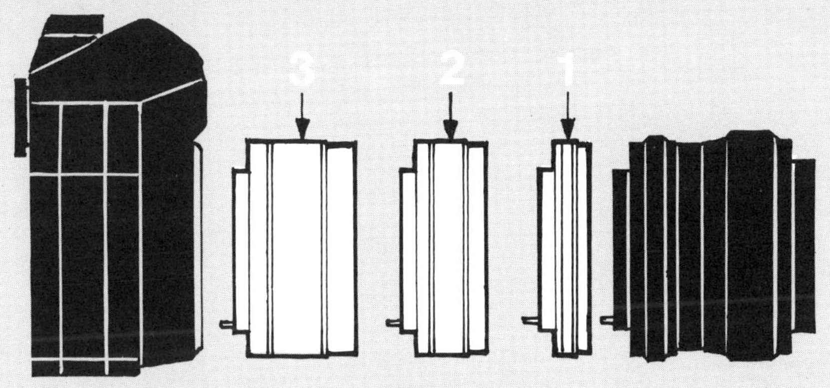

A

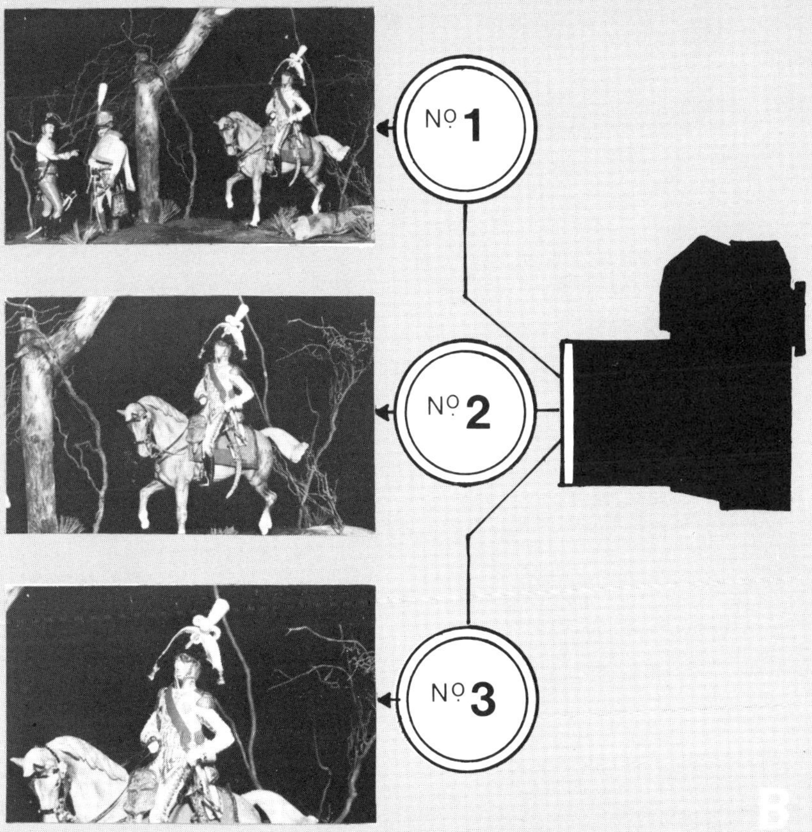

Nº 1

Nº 2

Nº 3

B

More sophisticated close-ups

Extension bellows

An extension bellows uses the same principle as tubes by adding extra extension behind the lens but it allows you to vary the extension continuously throughout the length of the collapsible bellows. Fuji provide a bellows of their own manufacture that gives, with a 55 mm lens, a range of magnifications from 0.61 to 2.32. The bellows is a simple but sturdy type giving a minimum extension of about 32 mm and a maximum of about 128 mm. The rail, which carries a scale of extensions, is mounted on a focusing block so that the required extension can be set and focusing carried out by moving the complete set-up back and forth.

To attach the bellows to the camera, you loosen the screw securing the camera mounting ring, which can then be removed and screwed into the camera body. You then push the camera body on to the bellows and tighten the screw. Be careful when removing the bellows. As you loosen the screw, the bellows falls off.

The lens is mounted on the front of the bellows in the normal way but it does not lock. The bellows has no full-aperture metering or auto diaphragm facilities. As you mount the lens, however, the auto-diaphragm pin is pushed in, converting the lens to a manual type.

You meter with the lens stopped down and, on the full-aperture-metering models, you must press the stop-down button on the camera front to obtain a correct reading, even though the lens is already stopped down. If you do not, the meter recommends much more exposure than you really need. It is best to lock the stop-down button in when using the bellows.

Reversing the lens

Camera lenses often given better results when they are reversed on bellows or tubes, so that the back of the lens faces the subject. Fuji supply a reverse adapter for this purpose. It screws into a filter thread of the camera lens and into the 42 mm thread of the lens mounting flange on camera, tube or bellows. There is also a Leica mount adapter for lenses with Leica thread.

Using a macro lens

There is one type of lens that is designed specifically for close-range work as well as normal photography. This is the so-called macro lens. The Fujinon macro lens is of 55 mm focal length and has extra extension built into its focusing travel to allow it to focus to 24 cm, where it provides an image about half life size. The size of the image is indicated directly on the lens distance scale.

The lens is also provided with an extension tube allowing life-size reproduction. In this case, the image size is indicated on the front of the focusing ring. Without the tube the lens can be used for full-aperture metering. With it, you have to meter with the lens stopped down. In both cases, however, it retains automatic diaphragm operation.

Close-up equipment

A Fuji Extension Bellows.
1 Camera mounting ring. **2** Securing screw. **3** Bellows. **4** Lens mount. **5** Focusing knob. **6** Extension scale. **7** Front standard clamp. **8** Focusing slide clamp.
B Fujinon 55mm macro lens.
1 Magnification with tube. **2** Focusing ring. **3** Magnification without tube. **4** Depth of field scale. **5** Aperture setting. **6** Extension tube for 1:1 reproduction. **7** Auto diaphragm pins.

1
2
3
4
5
6
7
8
A

∞ to 1/2 Actual Size
1/2 to Actual Size
With Tube (White)
Without Tube (Yellow)
1
2
3
4
5
6
7

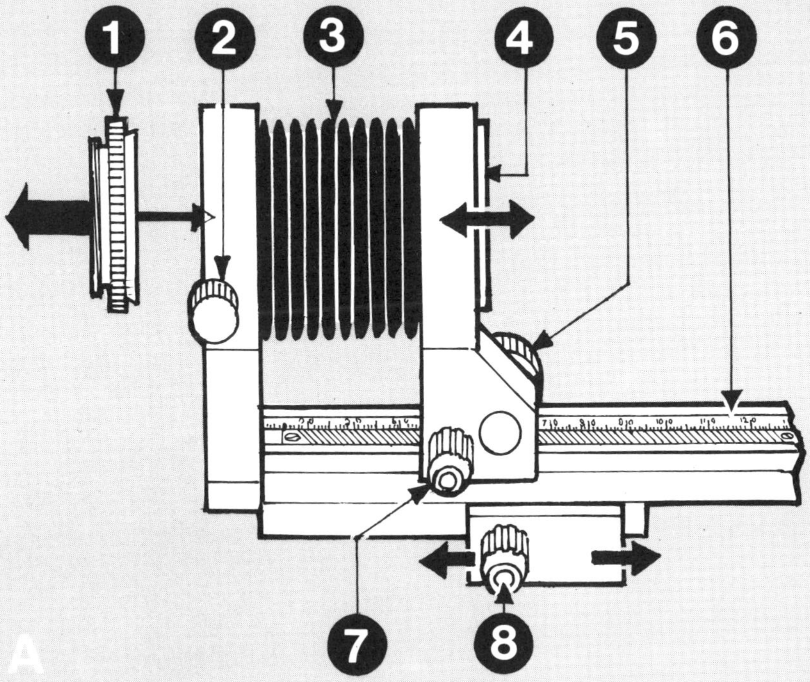

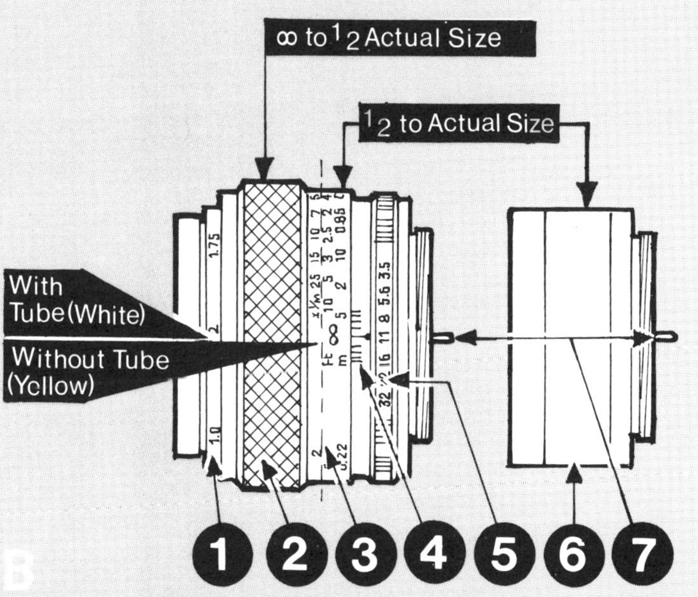

B

Working at ultra close range

Camera lenses are not well suited to really high-magnification work. This is the field of the microscope and photography of minute objects is best carried out with the microscope objective substituted for the camera lens. Fuji supply a microscope adapter for this purpose.

Microscope adapter

The adapter is an orthodox design with an extension tube to attach to the camera lens mount (the camera lens is not used) and a connecting ring attached to the microscope drawtube into which is slipped the microscope eyepiece or a light-shield tube when the eyepiece is not used.

The extension tube is fitted to the camera first and the connecting ring is clamped to the microscope drawtube after removing the eyepiece. The eyepiece can then be replaced or the light-shield tube can be substituted for it. The instructions tell you to insert the light-shield tube from the top but it appears, in fact, that it has to be inserted in the microscope tube before attaching the connecting ring. The camera and extension tube are then attached to the connecting tube by means of the connecting ring and the set-up is ready for use. A right-angle finder is useful for viewing and focusing.

Macrocine copier

An exceptional piece of close-range equipment for the Fujica cameras is the Macrocine Copier, designed for copying 8 mm or 16 mm cine frames on to the full 35 mm frame. Essentially it consists of a very small lens designed to work at an only slightly variable object distance but with provision for variable extension to provide different magnifications. The extension is provided by two tubes, both of which are used to enlarge an 8 mm frame to 35 mm, and a short helicoid for fine focusing. The film or other translucent item to be copied is held at a fixed distance from the lens (apart from the short helicoid travel) by a tubular copy head closed by a flat polished plate at the end with an 8 x 11 mm aperture. Sprung arms on this plate hold interchangeable aperture plates for 8 mm or 16 mm films, which are slid between the head plate and the aperture plate. The arms can also hold microscope slides or similar material.

Copying is carried out by pointing the camera with the unit attached toward a source of bright light, preferably sunlit sky. Metering can be effected by the camera meter but you can experience difficulty in seeing the needle of the 605 and 705. At the greater magnifications, exposure is very long unless powerful lamps are used and even the meter of the ST901 may not be able to cope. It might be better to put a diffuser over the movie frame and expose to electronic flash. You will then have to experiment to find the correct exposure.

The tubes supplied with the Macrocine Copier are of 19 and 28 mm focal length and can be used for close-ups with other lenses. They have no auto diaphgram mechanism.

Ultra close-up items

A Microscope adapter.
1 Extension tube. **2** Connecting tube. **4** Light shield tube. **5** Clamp. **6** Connecting ring. **7** Microscope eyepiece. **8** Microscope tube.
B Fuji Macrocinecopy
1 M–1 adapter ring. **2** M–2 adapter ring. **3** Focusing ring. **4** Copier head. **5** Aperture plate 8. **6** Aperture plate 16.

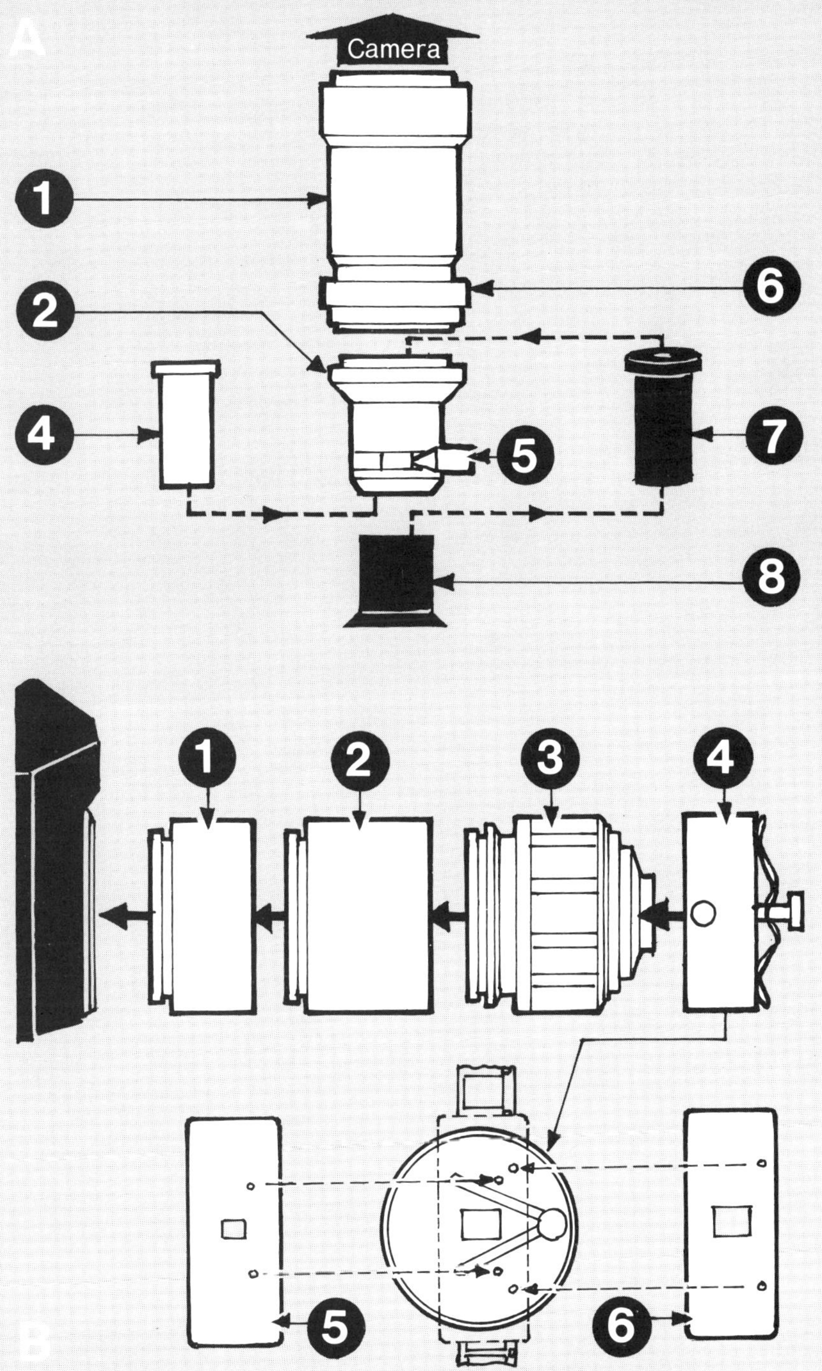
A
Camera
1
2
4
5
6
7
8
1
2
3
4
5
6
B

Useful accessories

Eyepiece attachments

The lens in the viewfinder eyepiece is a weak negative type so, if you are rather long-sighted, you might find it difficult to see the screen image clearly. Then you can have the lens changed to a positive type. Or, if you are very shortsighted and prefer to take your spectacles off to use your camera, you may like to change the lens for a stronger negative type. Fuji supply replacement lenses of +2, +0.5, –2.5 and –4 dioptres.

If you prefer to retain your spectacles, you will certainly find the rubber eyecup useful, especially with the ST901 and 801. It prevents light creeping past your eye into the viewfinder and dimming the LED readings with flare. It protects your spectacle lenses, too.

A further accessory to attach to the viewfinder eyepiece is the rightangle finder. This is a small, telescope-like attachment that can be rotated to allow you to view the whole screen image from above, below or to the side. It shows a laterally reversed image, which is a little off-putting when metering with the ST901 and trying to read the shutter speeds backward.

All the eyepiece accessories are in two versions, because the ST605 and 705 and the AZ-1 have rectangular eyepieces with grooves into which the attachments slide – leaving the eyepiece lens in place. The ST801 and 901 have screw-in eyepiece lenses that are removed for replacement or to fit the rightangle finder.

Other accessories

Among the other accessories supplied are lens hoods (also known as sunshades). The longer-focus lenses and zooms are supplied with hoods that slide forward for use. The fisheye has a very truncated hood attached. Accessory hoods are available for the 135, 100, 55, 50, 35 and 28 mm lenses, the last-mentioned being a rectangular type.

More vital, perhaps, are the lens caps and body caps supplied for all models and lenses. If you put your camera away with no lens attached, you run at least a slight danger of damaging the mirror. The body cap is designed to prevent that and to keep dust and other foreign bodies out of the camera. Similarly, any lens that is not in use should have caps back and front to protect the glass surfaces and the stop-down pin on the back of the lens mount.

All the cameras are supplied in so-called ever ready cases. Fuji's are no worse than others but they are clumsy and most people prefer to keep them for transport and storage rather than struggle with them while actually using the camera.

Fuji do not supply filters for their lenses except in the case of the 16 mm fisheye, which has four filters built in. Most of the Fuji lenses take 49 mm threaded filter mounts, however, so you have no difficulty in getting filters of various manufactures. You can even use the same size with the very long-focus lenses. They screw into the front of the lens mounting unit and are thus used behind the lens.

Filters and screens

Filters for mounting on camera lenses must be of the highest optical quality. There is no point in buying a specially coated lens accurately made from selected high quality glasses and then fitting over it a filter little better than a piece of window glass. Optical quality gelatin filters are ideal for occasional use, but are too delicate to be used continuously. For constant use glass filters (often a gelatin filter cemented between two pieces of glass) are essential. Filters manufactured for fitting over light sources (either photographic or theatrical) or in colour enlarger heads may produce distorted or degraded pictures if used on the camera. Intentional distortion may be introduced by using a dirty filter, or specially constructed lens attachments and screens. By such means, you can produce blurred images, flare, stars from bright points, multiple images and many other effects. Together with brightly coloured filters, these attachments play an important part in creative photography, but care should be taken to avoid accidentally emulating their effects. You should be specially careful of the condition and quality of a UV filter if, like many photographers, you keep it permanently in place.

Glass filters are supplied in rims which screw into the filter threads on the front of the lenses. The rims are manufactured in a standard range of sizes to suit most lenses. Adapter rings are available to allow the use of larger filters on lenses with smaller filter threads. Because of the standardization, you may be able to use one filter on several lenses, thus justifying the expense of buying a top quality filter.

As filters reduce the light reaching the film, they usually necessitate an increase in exposure time (or lens aperture). This increase is given as the *factor* by which the exposure time should be increased.

Aperture alterations can be calculated from this factor. Thus, for example, a 2× filter requires twice the exposure time or one stop larger aperture etc. Some manufacturers also give exposure increases in *thirds* of a stop. The simplest way of using these with a separate exposure meter (or one built into the camera which uses its own light window) is to decrease the film speed setting by one unit for each $\frac{1}{3}$ stop. Thus a $\frac{2}{3}$ stop increase would need an alteration from 80 ASA (20 DIN) to 50 ASA (18 DIN). Cameras with built-in through-the-lens meters also read through the filter, and thus give the correct exposure without any modification to the film setting. The meter can be used in its normal way.

Filters for black-and-white film

When they are used with black-and-white films UV and polarizing filters reduce haze and reflection respectively, just as they do with colour films. Coloured filters, however, affect the relative tonal rendering of different coloured parts of the subject. Because a filter acts by reducing the passage of light of complementary (opposite) colour, it reduces the image density produced on the negative from an object of that colour. The object thus comes out darker in the final print. If—as is usually the case—the camera exposure is increased to take account of the light absorbed by the filter, objects the same colour as the filter will be rendered lighter than normal in the final print.

The complements of red, green and blue are cyan (blue-green), magenta (red-purple) and yellow respectively; intermediate colours have intermediate complements. From this you can work out the colour of filter you need to give particular emphasis to any part of the subject. Yellow filters are widely used to darken blue parts of the subjects—in particular blue skies to emphasise white clouds.

Without any filter, blue parts of a subject tend to be rendered somewhat lighter than we see them because blue light tends also to contain some ultra-violet radiation, to which the film is sensitive, and the eye is not very sensitive to blue light. For this reason, a medium yellow filter may give a more natural tone rendering on panchromatic film, and is sometimes called a correction filter. The effect may be exaggerated by using a dark yellow or orange filter, or for greatest exaggeration a red filter. Such filters give increasingly darkened skies, with clouds standing out dramatically. The accepted "correction" filter for use with tungsten light is a yellow-green colour.

Because haze tends to reflect blue light and ultra-violet radiation in preference to green or red light, the use of yellow, red or orange filters can reduce its effect on the film. Deep red filters give the strongest haze penetration, but require considerable exposure increase, and of course affect the overall tonal rendering of the photograph.

Neutral density filters, naturally, do not affect the tone rendering. They simply allow you to increase the aperture or lengthen the shutter speed without overexposing the film.

Filters for colour photography

Filters are used in colour photography to alter the colour balance of the image on the film. Their use is mainly confined to reversal films because the colour balance of a print can be determined at the printing stage. Polarizing and ultra-violet absorbing filters, however, are commonly used with negative films as well.

Polarizing filters. The effect of a polarizing filter is the same with all types of film. It can—in some circumstances—reduce reflections; and can darken a blue sky, without otherwise altering the balance in a colour picture.

Light coming directly from the sun or other light source is not polarized: the rays vibrate in all directions. Sometimes, however, light can be restricted to rays all vibrating in one plane. It is then said to be polarized. For the photographer there are two important polarizers: polarizing filters, which restrict the passage of all light not vibrating in their plane of polarization; and smooth reflective non-metallic surfaces which polarize light reflected at certain angles. Although polarizing filters may be fitted over light-sources for special applications, they can normally be regarded as camera fitments used to take advantage of light polarized by reflection.

The most common use is in restricting the passage of polarized light, thus reducing its influence on the film. From certain angles this can result in a dramatic reduction in reflections from glass, water and similar substances (but not from metal surfaces). A special instance of this is the blue light reflected from the sky on a sunny day. An area of the sky at right angles to a line from the sun to the camera position polarises the sun's rays strongly, and thus careful use of a polarizing filter can selectively darken a blue sky in a colour picture.

The effect of a polarizing filter depends on its orientation to the polarized light. It passes almost all light polarized parallel to its polarizing plane, and is opaque to light polarized at right angles.

To simplify their use, polarizing filters for camera use are usually supplied in rotatable mounts. With a single lens reflex camera, you simply view the subject and rotate the filter until you see the effect you want. Some types also have a small extra filter on the rotation handle. This allows you to check the polarizing action independently of the main filter. Polarizing filters require an exposure increase of about $2\frac{1}{2}$ times ($1\frac{1}{3}$ stops).

Ultra-violet filters. Ultra-violet absorbing (UV) filters reduce the effect of atmospheric haze which would otherwise be exaggerated because photographic emulsions are sensitive to ultra-violet radiation (which is invisible to the eye). The radiation is scattered strongly by haze and records on colour film as a blue veiling of distant objects.

With colour reversal film an ultra-violet filter has the same haze-cutting effect, and also reduces the blue cast sometimes found in transparencies taken close to large reflecting masses such as water or snow. Such filters require no exposure increase.

Sky-light filters. Skylight filters are ultra-violet absorbing filters coloured a pale salmon or rose. They are used with reversal films to give slightly warmer colours in transparencies, as well as the normal UV filter effects. They require no exposure increase, and are a more useful alternative to plain UV filters.

Colour conversion filters. To obtain a normal colour balance when using a colour reversal film with a light source other than that for which it is intended to be used, you must use a coloured filter. Filters designed for this purpose are known as conversion filters. Many manufacturers supply them for using commonly available film types in normal types of illumination. In general, filters for use with daylight films are blue in colour, and those for use with artificial light films are orange. The filters are normally used on the camera lens, but are equally effective when used to filter the light-source. If you are to use two light sources of different colour temperatures, one of them must be filtered to the colour of the other.

Colour balancing filters. For special effects and for accurate colour matching, it may be necessary to change the colour balance slightly. Manufacturers supply two types of filter which are suitable: special pale filters designed for the purpose, and filters designed for colour printing. Almost invariably the necessity for particular filters can be determined only by testing, and information should be sought from the filter manufacturers.

Neutral density filters. Neutral density filters (or attenuators) reduce equally the transmission of all wavelengths of the visible spectrum. They come in two forms —*photographic silver density*, which is simply accurately exposed and developed film; and *dyed filters*—often using colloidal carbon. Because of its high light-scattering effect, silver density is not suitable for use over the camera lens. Dyed neutral density filters are, however, intended for this purpose, and can be used to produce high quality images.

Neutral density filters do not affect the colour balance whatever film they are used with. They simply allow the lens aperture to be widened, or the shutter speed lengthened, while restricting the exposure to its normal level. They are normally available in a range of densities from 0.1 to 4.0 (transmitting from 80% to 0.01% of the available light) with filter factors varying from just over 1 to 10,000. A density between 1.0 and 2.0 (10%–1% transmission) enables you to use full aperture in bright sun with medium speed films. A density of 3.0 (0.1% transmission) allows exposures up to 30 sec under the same conditions.

Colour principles

Shooting in colour is not significantly different from shooting in black and white. It is, in fact, possible for the newcomer in colour, already familiar with black and white photography, to become hypnotised by colour to such an extent that he forgets that his main aim is to produce a picture. He tends to introduce coloured objects into his picture or to search out colourful scenes. Those who start their photography in colour are not usually afflicted in this way.

Mood and perspective

Nevertheless, there are a few principles that it is as well to recognise. Colours do tend to have certain effects connected with mood and perspective. Colours in the reddish half of the spectrum give an impression of warmth, gaiety, garishness, danger, etc. according to the type of picture. The bluer colours are cooler, more sober, sometimes even depressing. Saturated colours are brash, brilliant, harsh, etc. whereas desaturated, pastel colours are delicate, soothing and soft. The bluer colours are less insistent and tend to sink into the background, while the redder colours tend to thrust forward and to attract the eye.

Colour harmony

We hear a lot about colour harmony, too, but this is a difficult subject on which to pontificate in photography. Where the picture is intended to be restful and soothing, it is a good general principle to include only colours that harmonise. But colour contrast and even clash is probably just as important. A certain amount of contrast is necessary in most pictures but the contrasting colour should generally be a relatively small part of the total scene—like the accessories in a lady's outfit.

In most pictures you accept the colours as they are but where any degree of contrivance is present or when you have reasonable control over the picture content there are a few points worth watching. Just as in black and white you should look for the obtrusive detail that has no relevance to the picture but in colour, you should pay particular attention where possible to red or other bright-coloured objects in the background. An outdoor portrait for example might be perfectly acceptable in black and white if a telephone kiosk or pillar box appeared out of focus in a small part of the background. In colour, such a defocused red blob would be distracting.

Similarly, any fussy background can generally be obscured in black and white by differential focusing. Colour backgrounds may still obtrude even when defocused.

Colour casts

Colour casts can be a problem. The black and white worker might be totally unprepared for the bluish features that can be produced by a wide-brimmed blue hat, the green reflected on to a white dress by grass or nearby foliage, or even the bright blue that can be reflected by snow from a brilliant blue sky.

An equally ineradicable cast can be produced by mixing light sources. There are colour films for use in daylight, others for use in artificial light and colour print films that are generally suitable for either type of lighting. No colour film, however, can render all colours accurately when exposed to both daylight or its equivalents and artificial light. The result is an orange-red cast in the parts of a daylight film affected by artificial light and a bluish cast in the parts of an artificial light film affected by daylight. Thus, if you use fill-in lighting you must use electronic flash, blue flash-bulbs or neutral coloured (preferably white) reflectors with daylight film and tungsten lighting or neutral-coloured reflectors with artificial light film. With colour print film, all your lighting must be of the same type or colour temperature.

Colour temperature

Films may be exposed to any light source, and—provided that they receive the correct exposure—will produce an image. Whatever the source, black-and-white films normally produce a satisfactory picture, but colour films require more carefully selected sources. The most important quality of a light source for colour photography is its colour. Everyday light varies from strong orange produced by household tungsten lamps to the pronounced blue of a clear blue sky—such as illuminates subjects in the shadow on a sunny day. Our eyes can compensate for different colours of overall lighting: we see white objects as white with any normal light source. Colour films, however, cannot compensate, and the colour balance of pictures is influenced by the colour of the light source.

The colour quality of light may be defined as its colour temperature. This is achieved by referring to the colour of light radiated by a theoretically perfect radiator heated to any particular temperature, which is measured in kelvins (K). Thus a light source radiating light of the same quality as the radiator at 5000 K is said to have a colour temperature of 5000 K. Low colour temperature (e.g. 2500 K) indicates a yellow or orange colour, and high colour temperature (e.g. 10 000 K) a blue colour.

Colour films

Colour films are balanced for particular light sources. Unless they are used with the right source, or the correct filter is used, they will not give a normal colour balance. For most purposes this is important only with reversal films—the colour balance of negatives can be corrected at the printing stage. Three types of reversal film are in common use: Daylight; type A, for use with 3400 K photolamps (over-run lamps such as Photofloods); and type B for use with 3200 K studio lamps or tungsten halogen lamps. Daylight type film is suitable for use with electronic flash (although a pale yellow filter is desirable with some units) and with blue coated flashbulbs.

Colour temperatures of some light sources

Light source	Colour temperature (K)
Skylight	12000–18000
Overcast sky	8000
Photographic 'white flame' carbon arc	7400
World average daylight	6500
Sunlight (noon)	5400
Daylight (sky and sun)	5500
English standard daylight	4800
Electronic flash	5500–7000
Blue coated flashbulb	6300
Flashcube and Magicube	4950
Low temperature carbon arc	4000
Clear flashbulb (aluminium filled)	3800
Photolamp 3400 K	3400
Tungsten studio lamp	3200
*Tungsten halogen lamp	3200
1000 watt & 500 watt floods	3000
General service bulb 200 watt	3000
General service bulb 100 watt	2900

* Photographic Studio type—others are variable

Fluorescent light sources do not always produce a continuous spectrum (i.e. light of all colours may not be equally represented), and give unpredictable results with colour films. After careful tests specially made "colour matching" tubes may prove satisfactory, but normal general service tubes are unlikely to give good pictures. When their use is unavoidable, a rough guide is to use daylight film and a red filter of the type designed for colour printing (about a 40R) with cold white tubes, and to use type B film (no filter) with warm white tubes.

The only way of ensuring accurate colour pictures when using an unknown combination of film and light source is to make a series of test exposures. For such a purpose you need a complete set of pale coloured filters—which must be of optical quality. Such filters are usually of real value only to the professional photographer.

Do not, however, be overcautious in matching even transparency films to light sources. For example, although you should use a pale blue filter, you can get quite acceptable results using unfiltered type B films with household lamps. In fact, some people prefer the warmer flesh-tones produced by this technique to correct colours. Slight over-exposure tends to minimize colour imbalance by lightening the overall density.

Mixed light sources

One very important factor, if you are to obtain an even colour balance overall, is to ensure that all the lighting used in one picture is the same colour temperature. This is just as important for colour negative films as it is for transparency films, because the colour balance of one part of a picture cannot be altered without altering the rest. The normal rule of thumb is that light sources should not differ in colour temperature by more than 100 K. Studio photographers use large pieces of filter in front of lights if they want to alter colour temperature. This is beyond most other photographers, but the use of small filters over electronic flash tubes can solve some problems. For example, using type A film an electronic flash could be mixed with photolamp (3400 K) illumination if the requisite (type A film used in daylight) filter were fitted over the flash head.

Glossary

Aberration. Failing in the ability of a lens to produce a true image. There are many forms of aberration and the lens designer can often correct some only by allowing others to remain. Generally, the more expensive the lens, the less its aberrations.

Angle of view. The extent of the view taken in by a lens. For any particular film size, it varies with the focal length of the lens. Usually expressed on the diagonal of the image area.

Aperture. The opening in the lens, usually provided by an adjustable iris diaphragm, though which light passes. See Limiting aperture, Effective aperture, *f*-number.

Aperture priority. Automatic exposure system in which the lens aperture is set by the photographer, and the camera sets the shutter speed. Can be used in the stop-down mode with any lens that does not interfere with the metering system.

Artificial light. Light from a man-made source, usually restricted to studio, photolamp and domestic lighting. When used to describe film (also known as Type A or Type B) invariably means these types of lighting.

ASA. Film speed rating defined by the American National Standards Institute.

Automatic iris. Lens diaphragm which is controlled by a mechanism in the camera body coupled to the shutter release. The diaphragm closes to any preset value before the shutter opens and returns to the fully open position when the shutter closes.

Balanced. Description applied to colour films to indicate their ability to produce acceptable colour response in various types of lighting. The films normally available are balanced for daylight (5500–6000K), photolamps (3400K) or studio lamps (3200K).

Cadmium sulphide (CdS). Photo conductive material used in exposure meters as alternative to selenium-based or silicon blue photocells. Its electrical resistance decreases as the light falling on it increases. Cds meters use current from an external power source, such as a battery.

Camera shake. Movement of camera caused by unsteady hold or support, vibration, etc., leading, particularly at slower shutter speeds, to a blurred image on the film. It is a major cause of unsharp pictures, especially with long focus lenses.

Capacitor. Electrical component once more commonly known as a condenser. Stores electrical energy supplied by a power source and can discharge it more rapidly than the source itself. Used in flash equipment, providing reliable bulb firing even from weak batteries, and supplying the surge needed for electronic flash tubes.

Cassette. Light-trapped film container used with 35 mm cameras.

Cast. Abnormal colouring of an image produced by departure from recommended exposure or processing conditions with a transparency film, or when making a colour print. Can also be caused by reflection within the subject as from a hat on to the face.

Click stop. Ball bearing and recess or similar construction used to enable shutter speeds, aperture values, etc. to be set by touch.

Colour negative. Film designed to produce colour image with both tones and colours reversed for subsequent printing to a positive image, usually on paper.

Colour reversal. Film designed to produce a normal colour positive image on the film exposed in the camera for subsequent viewing by transmitted light or projection on to a screen.

Colour temperature. Description of the colour of a light-source by comparing it with the colour of light emitted by a (theoretical) perfect radiator at a particular temperature expressed in kelvins (K). Thus "photographic daylight" has a colour temperature of about 5500K. Photographic tungsten lights have colour temperatures of either 3400K or 3200K depending on their construction.

Component. Part of a compound lens consisting of one element (single lens) or more than one element cemented or otherwise joined together. A lens may therefore be described as 4-element, 3-component when two of the elements are cemented together.

Computer flash. Electronic flash guns which sense the light reflected from the subject, and cut off their output when they have received sufficient light for correct exposure. Most units must be used on or close to the camera for direct lighting only, and the camera lens must be set to a specific aperture (or a small range of apertures) determined by the speed of the film in use.

Condenser. Generally a simple lens used to collect light and concentrate it on a particular area, as in enlarger or projector. Frequently in the form of two plano-convex lenses in a metal housing. A condenser, normally of the fresnel type, is used to ensure even illumination of the viewing screens on SLR cameras.

Contrast. Tonal difference. More often used to compare original and reproduction. A negative may be said to be contrasty if it shows fewer, more widely spaced tones than in the original.

Delayed action. Mechanism delaying the opening of the shutter for some seconds after the release has been operated. Also known as self-timer.

Depth of field. The distance between the nearest and farthest planes in a scene that a lens can reproduce with acceptable sharpness. Varies with effective aperture (and thus with focal length at any particular *f*-number) focused distance and the standards set for acceptable sharpness.

Developer. Solution used to make visible the image produced by allowing light to fall on the light-sensitive material. The basic constituent is a developing agent which reduces the light-struck silver halide to metallic silver. Colour developers include chemicals which produce coloured dyes coincidentally with reduction of the silver halides.

Diaphragm. Device consisting of thin overlapping metal leaves pivoting outwards to form a circular opening of variable size. Used to control light transmission through a lens.

DIN. Film speed rating defined by the Deutscher Normenausschuss (German standards organisation).

Effective aperture. The diameter of the bundle of light rays striking the first lens element that actually pass through the lens at any given diaphragm setting.

Electronic flash. Light source based on electrical discharge across two electrodes in a gas-filled tube. Usually designed to provide light approximating to daylight.

Element. Single lens used in association with others to form a compound construction.

Emulsion. Suspension of light-sensitive silver salts in gelatin.

Exposure. The act of allowing light to reach the light-sensitive emulsion of the photographic material. Also refers to the amount (duration and intensity) of light which reaches the film.

Exposure factor. A figure by which the exposure indicated for an average subject and/or processing should be multiplied to allow for non-average conditions. Usually applied to filters, occasionally to lighting, processing, etc. Not normally used with through-the-lens exposure meters.

Exposure meter. Instrument containing light sensitive substance which indicates aperture and shutter speed settings required.

Extension bellows. Device used to provide the additional separation between lens and film required for close-up photography. Consists of extendible bellows and mounting plates at front and rear to fit the lens and camera body respectively.

Extension tubes. Metal tubes used to obtain the additional separation between lens and film for close-up photography. They are fitted with screw thread or bayonet mounts to suit various lens mounts.

***f*-number.** Numerical expression of the light-transmitting power of a lens. Calculated from the focal length of the lens divided by the diameter of the bundle of light rays entering the lens and passing through the aperture in the iris diaphragm.

Film base. Flexible support on which light sensitive emulsion is coated.

Filter. A piece of material which restricts the transmission of radiation. Generally coloured to absorb light of certain colours. Can be used over light sources or over the camera lens. Camera lens filters are usually glass—either dyed or sandwiching a piece of gelatin—in a screw-in filter holder.

Fisheye lens. Ultra-wide angle lens giving 180° angle of view. Basically produces a circular image—on 35 mm, 5–9 mm lenses showing whole image, 15–17 mm lenses giving a rectangular image fitting just inside the circle, thus representing 180° across the diagonal.

Fixer. Solution, usually based on sodium thiosulphate, in which films or prints are immersed after development to convert the unexposed silver halides in the emulsion to soluble products that can be washed out. This prevents subsequent deterioration of the image.

Flashbulb. Light source based on ignition of combustible metal wire in a gas-filled transparent envelope. Popular sizes are usually blue-coated to give light approximating to daylight.

Flashcube. Self-contained unit comprising four small flashbulbs with own reflectors. Designed to rotate in special camera socket as film is wound on. Can be used in a special adapter on cameras without the socket, but will not rotate automatically.

Focal length. Distance from a lens to the image it produces of a very distant subject. With a compound lens the point from which it is measured depends on the construction of the lens. It is within the lens with those of normal construction, but may be in front of telephoto lenses, or behind inverted telephotos. Whatever the lens construction, the focal length determines the size of the image formed.

Focus. Generally, the act of adjusting a lens to produce a sharp image. In a camera, this is effected by moving the lens bodily towards or away from the film or by moving the front part of the lens towards or away from the rear part, thus altering its focal length.

Format. Shape and size of image provided by camera or presented in final print or transparency. Governed in the camera by the opening at the rear of the body over which the film passes or is placed. The standard 35 mm format is 36 × 24 mm; half-frame, 18 × 24 mm; 126 size, 28 × 28 mm; 110, 17 × 13 mm; standard rollfilm (120 size), $2\frac{1}{4} \times 2\frac{1}{4}$ in.

Fresnel. Pattern of a special form of condenser lens consisting of a series of concentric stepped rings, each being a section of a convex surface which would, if continued, form a much thicker lens. Used on focusing screens to distribute image brightness evenly over the screen.

Full aperture metering. TTL metering systems in which the camera simulates the effect of stopping down the lens when the aperture ring is turned, while leaving the diaphragm at full aperture to give full focusing screen brilliance. The meter must be "programmed" with the actual full aperture, and the diaphragm ring setting.

Grain. Minute metallic silver deposit, forming in quantity the photographic image. The individual grain is never visible, even in an enlargement, but the random nature of their distribution in the emulsion causes overlapping, or clumping, which can lead to graininess in the final image.

Graininess. Visible evidence of the granular structure of a photographic reproduction. Influenced by exposure, development, contrast characteristics and surface of printing paper, emulsion structure and degree of enlargement. Basically increases with increasing film speed.

Grey card. Tone used as representative of mid-tone of average subject. The standard grey card reflects 18 per cent of the light falling on it.

Guide number. Figure allocated to a light source, usually flash, representing the product of aperture number and light-to-subject distance required for correct exposure.

Halation. The production of "halos" round bright spots in an image, by light reflecting from the back of the film-base. General film bases are given a light-absorbing coat—the anti-halation back—to prevent this.

Highlight. Small, very bright part of image or object. Highlights should generally be pure white, although the term is sometimes used to describe the lightest tones of a picture, which, in that case, may need to contain some detail.

Image. Two-dimensional reproduction of a subject formed by a lens. When formed on a surface, i.e. a ground-glass screen, it is a real image; if in space, i.e. when the screen is removed, it is an aerial image. The image seen through a telescope, optical viewfinder, etc. cannot be focused on a surface without the aid of another optical system and is a virtual image.

Incident light. Light falling on a surface as opposed to the light reflected by it.

Infinity. Infinite distance. In practice, a distance so great that any object at that distance will be reproduced sharply if the lens is set at its infinity position, i.e. one focal length from the film.

Interchangeable lens. Lens designed to be readily attached to and detached from a camera.

Inverted telephoto lens. Lens constructed so that the back focus (distance from rear of lens to film) is greater than the focal length of the lens. This construction allows room for mirror movement when short focus lenses are fitted to SLR cameras.

Iris. Strictly, iris diaphragm. Device consisting of thin overlapping metal leaves pivoting outwards to form a circular opening of variable size to control light transmission through a lens.

Leader. Part of film attached to camera take-up spool. 35 mm film usually has a leader of the shape originally designed for bottom-loading Leica cameras, although most cameras simply need a short taper.

Lighting ratio. The ratio of the brightness of light falling on the subject from the main (key) light and other (fill) lights. A ratio of about 3:1 is normal for colour photography, greater ratios may be used for effect in black-and-white work.

Limiting aperture. The actual size of the aperture formed by the iris diaphragm at any setting. Determines, but usually differs from, the effective aperture.

Long-focus. Lens of relatively long focal length designed to provide a narrower angle of view than the normal or standard lens, which generally has an angle of view, expressed on the diagonal of the film format, of about 45 deg. The long focus lens thus takes in less of the view in front of it but on an enlarged scale.

Magicube. Special form of flashcube which is fired by mechanical (not electrical) means. Can be used only on cameras fitted with the appropriate socket.

Manual iris. Diaphragm controlled directly by a calibrated ring on the lens barrel.

Microprism. Minute glass or plastic structure of multiple prisms set in a viewfinder screen to act as a focusing aid. Breaks up an out-of-focus subject into a shimmer but images a focused subject clearly. Will not work satisfactorily at lens apertures smaller than *f* 5·6.

Mirror lens. Lens in which some (usually two) of the elements are curved mirrors. This construction produces comparatively lightweight short fat long focus lenses. They cannot be fitted with a normal diaphragm.

Modelling. Representation by lighting of the three-dimensional nature of an original in a two-dimensional reproduction.

Neutral density filter. Grey filter that absorbs light of all colours equally and thus has no effect on colour rendering with colour film or tonal values with black and white film. Primarily used with mirror lenses or to enable large apertures to be used in bright light conditions.

Parallax. Apparent change in position of an object due to changed viewpoint. In a camera with separate viewfinder, the taking lens and the viewfinder view an object from slightly different positions. At close range, the image produced on the film is significantly different from that seen in the viewfinder. Completely eliminated in single-lens reflex cameras.

Perspective. Size, position and distance relationship between objects. Varies according to viewpoint so that objects at different distances from the observer, appear to be closer together with increasing distance. Thus, a long-focus lens used at long range and a wide-angle lens used very close up provide images very different from that of the standard lens used at a normal working distance.

Photolamp (3400K). Photographic lamp giving more light than a normal lamp of the same wattage, at the expense of filament life. Often referred to by the trade mark Photoflood. Are used with type A colour films.

Plane. Level surface. Used in photography chiefly in respect to focal plane, an imaginary level surface perpendicular to the lens axis in which the lens is intended to form an image. When the camera is loaded the focal plane is occupied by the film surface.

Polarized light. Light waves vibrating in one plane only as opposed to the multi-directional vibrations of normal rays. Natural effect produced by some reflecting surfaces, such as glass, water, polished wood, etc., but can also be simulated by placing a special screen in front of the light source. The transmission of polarized light is restricted by using a screen at an angle to the plane of polarization.

Preset iris. Diaphragm with two setting rings or one ring that can be moved to two positions. One is click-stopped, but does not affect the iris, the other moves freely and alters the aperture. The required aperture is preset on the first ring, and the iris closed down with the second just before exposure.

Rangefinder. Instrument for measuring distances from a given point, usually based on slightly separated views of the scene provided by mirrors or prisms. May be built into non-reflex cameras. Single-lens reflexes may have prismatic rangefinders built into their focusing screens.

Refill. Length of film usually for loading into 35 mm cassettes in total darkness. Daylight refills are not now generally available.

Relative aperture. Numerical expression of effective aperture, also known as *f*-number. Obtained by dividing focal length by diameter of effective aperture.

Resolution. Ability of film, lens or both in conjunction to reproduce fine detail. Commonly measured in lines per millimetre as ascertained by photographing, or focusing the lens on, a specially constructed test target. The resolution of modern lenses and films is so high that differences have no bearing on normal photography except with the simplest lenses and fastest films.

Safelight. Light source consisting of housing, lamp and screen of a colour that will not affect the photographic material in use. Safelight screens are available in various colours and sizes for specific applications.

Scale. Focusing method consisting of set of marks to indicate distances at which a lens is focused. May be engraved around the lens barrel, on the focusing control or on the camera body.

Screen. In a camera, the surface upon which the lens projects an image for viewfinding and, usually, focusing purposes. In SLR cameras, almost universally a fresnel screen with a fine-ground surface. Often incorporates a microprism or split-image rangefinder.

Selenium. Light-sensitive substance which, when used in a barrier-layer construction, generates electrical current when exposed to light. Used in exposure meters. Needs no external power supply.

Self-timer. Mechanism delaying the opening of the shutter for some seconds after the release has been operated. Also known as delayed action.

Semi-automatic iris. Diaphragm mechanism which closes down to the taking aperture when the shutter is released, but must be manually re-opened to full aperture.

Sensitivity. Expression of the nature of a photographic emulsion's response to light. Can be concerned with degree of sensitivity as expressed by film speed or response to light of various colours (spectral sensitivity).

Sharpness. Clarity of the photographic image in terms of focus and contrast. Largely subjective but can be measured to some extent by assessing adjacency effects, i.e. the abruptness of the change in density between adjoining areas of different tone value.

Short-focus. Lens of relatively short focal length designed to provide a wider angle of view than the normal or standard lens, which generally has an angle of view, expressed on the diagonal of the film format, of about 45 deg. The short focus lens takes in more of the view in front of it but on a smaller scale.

Shutter priority. Automatic exposure systems in which the shutter speed is set by the photographer, and the camera selects the lens aperture appropriate to the film speed and the light reflected from the subject. Such systems must meter the light at full aperture and use specially connected lenses.

Silicon. Light-sensitive substance which generates a minute current when exposed to light. Requires no external power source, but, in exposure meters, uses an externally powered amplifier.

Split-image. Form of rangefinder image, bisected so that the two halves of the image are aligned only when the correct object distance is set on the instrument or, in the case of a coupled rangefinder, when the lens is correctly focused. SLR cameras may have a prismatic split-image system in their viewing screen. Works on the same principle as a microprism, and is restricted to apertures of *f* 5·6 or greater.

Stabilizer. Alternative to fixer where permanence is not required. Used in automatic processing machines and can now provide prints that will not deteriorate noticeably over many months if kept away from strong light.

Stop-down metering. TTL metering in which the light is measured at the picture-taking aperture. As the meter just measures the light passing through the lens, there is no need for any lens-camera interconnections.

Studic lamps (3200K). Tungsten or tungsten halogen lamps designed for studio use. Have a longer life than photolamps, but a lower specific output and colour temperature. Are used with type B films.

Supplementary lens. Generally a simple positive (converging) lens used in front of the camera lens to enable it to focus at close range. The effect is to provide a lens of shorter focal length without altering the lens-film separation, thus giving the extra extension required for close focusing.

Synchronisation. Concerted action of shutter opening and closing of electrical contacts to fire a flashbulb or electronic flash at the correct moment to make most efficient use of the light output. Roughly speaking, FP or M-synchronisation is constructed to fire flashbulbs just before the shutter is fully open, allowing a build-up time, and X-synchronisation fires electronic flash exactly at the moment the shutter is fully open.

Telephoto. Special form of long-focus lens construction in which the back focus (distance from rear of lens to film) is much less than the focal length of the lens.

Through-the-lens (TTL). Type of exposure meter built into the camera body and reading through the camera lens. May measure either at full aperture or at picture taking aperture.

Type A. Colour film balanced for use with photolamps (3400K).

Type B. Colour film balanced for use with studio lamps (3200K).

Ultra-wide angle lens. Extra-wide angle lens, usually those with an angle of view greater than 90°. For 35 mm cameras the description usually applies to lenses of shorter focal length than about 24 mm.

Variable focus lens. Lens of which the focal length can be continuously varied between set limits. The lens must be refocused with each change in focal length.

Viewfinder. Device or system indicating the field of view encompassed by the camera lens. The term is sometimes used as a description of the type of camera that does not use reflex or "straight-through" viewing systems and therefore has to have a separate viewfinder.

Vignetting. Underexposure of image corners produced deliberately by shading or unintentionally by inappropriate equipment, such as unsuitable lens hood or badly designed lens. A common fault of wide-angle lenses, owing to reflection, cut-off, etc. of some of the very oblique rays. May be caused in some long-focus lenses by the length of the lens barrel.

Wide-angle. Lens designed to provide a wider angle of view than the normal or standard lens. Generally has an angle of view, expressed on the diagonal of the film format, of about 60 deg. or more. The wide-angle lens thus takes in more of the view in front of it but on a reduced scale.

Zoom lens. Lens of which the focal length can be continuously varied within stated limits while maintaining the focus originally set.